intuitive
REBEL

intuitive
REBEL

tuning in to the voice that matters

CHARLES HOLT

Foreword by Michael Bernard Beckwith

Agape Media International

Agape Media International
Los Angeles, California

Agape Media International

Published by Agape Media International, LLC
5700 Buckingham Parkway
Culver City, CA 90230
310.258.4401
www.agapeme.com

HAY
HOUSE

Distributed by Hay House, Inc.
Hay House USA
P.O. Box 5100, Carlsbad, CA 92018-5100
760.431.7695 or 800.654.5126
www.hayhouse.com®

Hay House UK: www.hayhouse.co.uk
Hay House Australia: www.hayhouse.com.au
Hay House South Africa: www.hayhouse.co.za
Hay House India: www.hayhouse.co.in

Intuitive Rebel
Charles Holt

Foreword by Michael Bernard Beckwith
Editor: Kuwana Haulsey
Initial Edit by: Kevin Anderson
Cover Photos: Kevin McIntyre
Book Cover and Interior Design: Pip Abrigo
Executive in Charge of Publication: Stephen Powers

Printed in USA on recycled paper

ISBN: 978-1-4019-4032-4

Acknowledgments

My grandmother, Wilhelmina S. Holt, was the embodiment of this great Presence that many choose to call God. Through her willingness and availability to allow Spirit to reveal and demonstrate Itself through and as her, I too am encouraged to do the same. To my mother, who is my hero and best friend, I thank you for always loving me without reservation and for giving me permission to be all that I came to be. To my father, I am grateful for you teaching me how to live my life according to how I believe and not what others may believe about me. To my brother, I am grateful for the gift of courage to accomplish dreams I thought too difficult to take on and the perseverance to finish the task. To my dear sister who helped raise and care for me. I remember you teaching me how to count in Spanish and introducing me to a world of possibilities. I praise my teachers, coaches, and mentors: Reverend S. H. Simpson for being a great storyteller; Coach Fred Hill for believing that I could become a world-class sprinter and athlete; Alyce S. McDowell for showing me how to hold on to the values of excellence; Patdro Harris for seeing gifts and talents in me that I was blind to; Carl Anderson for teaching me how to illuminate the Broadway stage; to Rickie Byars Beckwith for playing in the key of life and giving me, once again, a glimpse of the glory of music; and to Dr. Michael Beckwith, my friend and Spiritual Advisor, who through one spoken word opened my soul up to remember who and what I really am, and why I came to the planet at this particular time. I thank Stephen Powers at Agape Media International for believing in my work and for all of the support in helping me share my dream with people around the world. Thank you also to Mark Harris for being a vital part of the AMI intention. I appreciate your kind words and the work you have done to inspire the world. I appreciate Ben Dowling for his acts of service and for his efforts in creating marketing platforms, so that the work becomes a blessing to people everywhere. To my friend, Freda Buford, who held my hand while I sang my first solo in church. And to my ancestors who held the high watch and saw it unfold from the beginning. I am forever grateful.

Love,

Charles Holt

Contents

Foreword by Michael Bernard Beckwith • *1*

Chapter 1: *Cleaning Up Your Mental Garbage* • *5*

Chapter 2: *The Seed of Conscious Choice* • *19*

Chapter 3: *Learning How to Listen Again* • *35*

Chapter 4: *Losing Your Dreams, Gaining Yourself* • *51*

Chapter 5: *Silencing the Angry Voices* • *63*

Chapter 6: *Stepping Into the Unknown* • *80*

Chapter 7: *Let's Be Honest* • *94*

Chapter 8: *Having the Courage to Surrender,*
to Shine, and to Share • *107*

Chapter 9: *Making Choices* • *120*

Chapter 10: *Putting It to Practice* • *137*

Chapter 11: *The Healing Power of Forgiveness* • *145*

Chapter 12: *The Beauty of Release* • *157*

Chapter 13: *Love: What It All Boils Down To* • *171*

Chapter 14: *The Voice Will Always Remind Us*
of Who and What We Are • *187*

Chapter 15: *And the Two Shall Become One* • *200*

By Michael Bernard Beckwith

The voice of Charles Holt brings to my mind these words of the great Sufi teacher, Hazrat Inayat Khan, "The voice is not only indicative of a man's character, but it is the expression of his spirit. His voice will tell you how far he has evolved... the etheric quality of the voice is inspiring, healing, peace giving, harmonizing, convincing, appealing; at the same time it is most intoxicating."

The vibrant song of life that sings itself through and as the spirit of Charles Holt exquisitely echoes throughout the book you hold in your hands. In language that is both fierce and tender, Charles's journey is a potent affirmation of how the limitless possibilities that lie within you, and within all beings, may become fully realized. It has required great inner strength to be so forthright, so publicly self-revealing about the intimate details of his path that make this book so valuable to its readers. And yet it is no surprise to me, because from our first meeting it was easy to see Charles's authenticity, which is a hallmark of his nature.

I well remember the Sunday in 2005 when Charles first approached and greeted me. Imagine my surprise when, not knowing at all why, I found myself placing my one hand on his shoulder, taking his hand in my other and saying, "You should start journaling." Although his response wasn't verbal, his facial response and body language said it all: *What is this guy talking about? These aren't the words of wisdom I expected to hear after waiting in line all this time!* Later he confided to me how resistant he felt to this suggestion, and that it lasted until during one of his meditation sessions when an inner voice intimated, "Write down what comes to you in meditation, in your daily experiences." Following that inner admonition has resulted in the pages that fill *Intuitive Rebel.*

I have had the blessing of Charles's friendship long enough to have witnessed the evolution of his talents as an artist. As a student of mine in classes and member of my congregation, I have factual evidence of how, as a person's spirit deepens, the healing qualities of his gifts and skills express in direct proportion to his expansion of consciousness and communion with inspiration's Source. Heaven breathes itself through Charles' artistic gifts, and I have no doubt that his readers will find their hearts being opened by his intuitive depths, his generosity of heart, his authenticity in walking the spiritual warrior's path.

The theme of individual inner freedom is an apparent quality of Charles's and can be felt throughout his artistic expressions and performances. It is, in fact, one of his most contagious qualities. A taste for authentic freedom will no doubt infect his readers to cultivate the same within themselves. But this is just one of the many gifts he offers. Perhaps the most vital is Charles's conviction that what he has demonstrated through his victorious journey is possible to anyone who perseveres in applying spiritual principles to discover and manifest his or her life's purpose. The courage and trust he exhibited leaving Atlanta, Georgia, with only $400 in his pocket and heading for the bright lights of Broadway resulted in his performing before sold-out audiences throughout the world including at the John

F. Kennedy Center and the Turkish-American Association in Ankara, Turkey. While this is certainly impressive in itself, it is the spiritual tools Charles activated within himself that lighted his path to such inner and outer success.

Through sharing his inner journey, Charles humbly and enthusiastically invites his readers to embark on realizing their highest potential, to live their dreams, to fulfill their purpose. It is an invitation in which the reader may have complete confidence.

Chapter 1

Cleaning Up Your Mental Garbage

The First Time I Heard the Voice

I sat behind my desk staring at the letter in my hand, as if I could somehow will the words in front of me to change, to become less painful and devastating.

Letter of Termination …

I was one of the top sales reps in the entire company, one of the best in Atlanta, and I was getting fired. The only thing I could think was how am I going to tell my mother?

She was still distraught over my departure from the sales department at IBM—a stable, good paying, high-profile job. As much as I hated to admit it, she had good reason to be upset. At that point, my life was in shambles. Creditors were relentlessly breathing down my neck. I'd made lots of money but hadn't been the best steward over my finances. Proper budgeting hadn't been a high priority, and I was feeling the harsh repercussions. Now I wouldn't even have a steady paycheck coming in. In my head, the voices of my family members, friends, and neighbors created a deafening chorus that started with I told you so and ended with I knew it! The voices grew louder and louder until it felt nearly impossible to shut them out. Unfortunately, the most strident and judgmental voice in the pack was my own. I ended up calling my close friend Patdro first to tell him the bad news. His response was not at all what I expected. It stunned me enough to get my full attention. "Good!" he crowed. "I'm glad you got fired! Now you can start doing what you're supposed to be doing." "And what am I supposed to be doing?" I asked, kind of peeved that he refused to join my pity party. "You're a performer, Charles," Patdro said. "Your gift is quite apparent. You really touch and move people in a special way when you're on stage."

When Patdro said you're a performer, something bolted awake inside me. I now recognize that his words were the voice of Spirit, speaking to me in the only way that I was able to receive it at the time. Back then it made absolutely no sense. But, sensible or not, I couldn't get away from the joy and excitement that I felt inside when I listened to my friend make that pronouncement.

I'd been singing at open mic nights in local jazz clubs on the weekends. It was nothing major. Singing and acting were just things I did for fun. The idea of doing it professionally was so outside the box that my rational mind couldn't even take the thought seriously. The dream of performing had been buried so deep within me that I didn't even know I had it inside. All I knew was that there was something about the whole idea that just felt right. My soul had heard, and recognized, the truth.

Taking Patdro's advice, I walked away from the corporate world and enrolled in my first acting class, a beginner's class held on Saturday for a couple of hours at a time. I felt like I was back in kindergarten at St. Bartholomew School in Nashville, learning to swing on the monkey bars. At the end of the three-week class, both instructors, BJ Hughes and Marion Walton, told me that I had a gift and should be auditioning for roles, echoing what Patdro had said.

I had a gift? I was a natural? This was a very heady thing to hear for a corporate sales representative.

Even though I wasn't ready to acknowledge it at that point, I was starting to figure out what I was down here on Earth to do. I still had no idea what it would end up looking like. But somehow I knew that my mentors were right—I had to sing. I would sing even if I got no recognition and no money, which is exactly what happened at first.

I sang at weddings and other events for absolutely no money for quite a while. I didn't ask to be paid for my service and neither did anyone offer. At that point, I didn't know any better. I just knew that there was something about singing and performing that gave me a joy that nothing on the outside could touch. This new path baffled my mother, my family and most of my friends. But even that didn't matter.

My first professional acting gig was a community theater piece that wouldn't pay for a week's worth of groceries. I was ecstatic. There was something inherent in performing that fed the lifeline inside me, which said, keep coming! If you keep traveling down this road, I'll show you why you're here. Following my heart opened me up to experience the joy and freedom that came along with being fully engaged with my purpose. It was pure bliss, unlike anything I'd known.

Eventually, I was cast in the Alliance Theatre's production of

The Amen Corner. This opportunity to perform on the main stage at one of the most respected regional theaters in the country was the first step of an almost mystical unfolding of the Universal good. The show ran for a month: packed houses, standing ovations, and hands clapping; people filled the aisles singing, dancing, and rejoicing in "hallelujah" happiness. Joy filled the building. During one particular evening performance, I went to my dressing room at intermission as a part of my usual routine. I sighed as I sat down, glancing into the mirror at my dressing-room table.

Suddenly I heard a voice say, "It's time."

I looked around to see if anybody else was in the room, but I was alone.

I became very still, trying to figure out where the voice was coming from and to whom it belonged. It sounded vaguely familiar, yet I didn't recognize it. It was unlike any voice that I'd ever heard in my life, a sort of mysterious, "spacey" sound. Just as I was beginning to think I might be working too hard, the voice spoke once again.

"It is time."

I wasn't totally clueless in understanding what these words meant. I'd recently met Adrian Bailey, a seasoned actor who was in town doing a production of *Boys from Syracuse.* He'd been on his way back to New York for the premiere of *Smokey Joe's Cafe,* in which he starred. Adrian encouraged me to listen to the music from the show. So for months I'd been listening to the soundtrack and, without telling anyone, I'd made up my mind to go to New York to audition for one of the roles.

After I heard the voice, I no longer hesitated with my

decision. Nor did I think too much or too hard about making such a profound move. Somehow, I knew the voice had come to me as a divine guide and to give me direction. I just declared it a done deal and purchased my airline ticket as soon as I could.

I said yes to the voice and left the details up to the Universe.

On July 6, 1996, two months after *The Amen Corner* closed, I left Atlanta and life in the South, which was all I'd ever known. With $400 in my pocket and a conviction that "something" was leading me down this unfamiliar road, I headed off to a new life in New York City.

Although I didn't have a clue what to expect I was certain that something greater than anything I'd ever known or experienced awaited me. What I didn't realize was that I was about to embark on an adventure so profound that it would reshape my entire view of reality and the spiritual threads that connect us all.

Recognizing the Good Stuff

The voice, as I call it, is a spontaneous demonstration from the Source that speaks directly to the divine nature within an individual. I speak of it as a "voice" because it articulates the truth of universal awareness. Held within this awareness are the answers to any question you could possibly have about yourself, your life, and your purpose here on this planet. The voice of truth within us is what leads us away from religious dogma and into authentic spiritual awakening. Innovation, inspiration, creative genius, truth, and intuitive wisdom all stem from our ability to receive and act on the guidance of our inner voice.

The voice can come to us in many ways. It can be heard, like I heard it that night in my dressing room. It can be felt, smelled, or simply intuited. For some people, the voice can even speak through colors, which bring back memories. So, for example, when I see the iridescent green wings of a hummingbird flying by, I think spring in Tennessee. Then I remember something that my grandmother said that I hadn't thought about in years. She told me that green stood for plentitude. And if I feel that there's lack or scarcity in my life, the message of the hummingbird will resonate with me in a way that inspires open awareness. My memory, through my grandmother, has spoken something necessary to me. What has been declared across time and space has come to the center of my being to speak life. Now, when I think I'm in lack, the voice says, "What did mygrandmother tell me? Green means plentitude. It means lush. It means volume. It means wealth. And if my grandmother said it, I can believe it. Look around. Green is everywhere. I'm surrounded byabundance everywhere I go." There's an intimate space where that particular voice will resonate.

No matter what we see or what we feel out in the day-to-day world, there's always that gentle but persistent voice within that speaks of life. When we access the voice and begin to converse with it, we're actually creating a platform where we hear, feel, and experience life as a world of possibility.

Coming to Terms with the Not-So-Good Stuff

The process of accessing your intuitive voice may seem like it should be a simple one. And for some people it is. But for many others, perhaps most of us, the process is anything but clear or simple. Issues arise for those who have, to varying degrees, become disconnected from themselves and their authentic desires over the years. For these people, it may seem next to impossible to discern the voice of guidance from the chattering voices of fear, doubt, lack, and worry. The imposter voices (derived from the ego) speak confusion and unhappiness into situations, rather than calling forth truth, courage and light. They spew mental garbage over your dreams. They often sound exactly like the authority figures who have exerted control over you throughout your life, especially in your childhood.

I know this from firsthand experience.

When I was a child, I saw life as exciting and fresh, with something new to discover at every turn. Like all children, I believed that anything was possible. But then one beautiful summer afternoon when I was 5 years old, two of my parents' friends came to visit.

Even though the couple lived in our neighborhood, just one street away, it wasn't often that they came over for a formal visit. Everybody knew everybody else in the small community, so people always stopped to talk whenever they passed by each other's doorsteps. But having someone over for dinner was a rare treat.

These occasions were always a favorite time of mine. Being the youngest of three, I'd grown accustomed to being the center of attention. And this was the perfect time for me to show off my dancing skills. The antique lamps in the living room were all turned on, signaling that our company had arrived. I could hear my mother greeting the guests at the door. I had my little, square record player and my 45 of the Jackson 5's "Rockin' Robin" all set to play. As soon as our guests stepped into our living room, I started dancing all over the house, pantomiming as I went along.

With my dingy, tattered bed blanket draped around my shoulder, I did all the latest and hippest moves that came to mind—many of which I'd learned from watching *Soul Train* on Saturdays—always ending my combination with a James Brown split. After starting "my show" in the living room, I shuffled into the kitchen and then into the bathroom. I made a grand re-entry into the living room with a handspring into a push up and then the popular "robot." They loved it!

"Look at him get down!"

"Work it out, lil man!"

I basked in the applause and in the pride of watching my mother's eyes light up in amazement. The more they encouraged me, the faster I moved. My feet felt light as a feather, and my body jerked and gyrated in total surrender to the rhythm. I became lost to the world around me.

As my parents' friends stood enthralled, waiting with great anticipation for the climax of the performance, I began my finale. But then, without warning, my father stepped briskly into the room. I met his eyes and in an instant sensed his anger and complete disapproval.

"Shut that music off!" he snapped. "Get in your room right now! All of that silly dancing and performing is uncalled for.

Now go!" And of course, the exclamation came with the age-old southern adage, "You are a child, and children have no business being in grown folks' business!"

I was crushed! Too startled to breathe and too humiliated to cry, I quickly gathered my things and rushed to my room, throwing myself onto the bed and covering my entire body with my blanket.

In that moment, dancing and all of what I had loved so much about this fun and free artistic expression became wrong and unachievable in my mind. That experience struck such fear in me that it stopped me from performing altogether. The possibility of evoking that type of reaction again was too awful to risk. Yet, I didn't understand how something that gave others such joy and happiness could be wrong. I thought, maybe only certain people are allowed to be themselves in any way they want to. Perhaps I looked stupid and awkward dancing, and my father's reprimand was his way of protecting me from future embarrassment. I concluded that no matter what the reason, performing was not for me. My father's words affected me so deeply that it changed the course of my life for the next 20 years.

Inspired Thought vs. Uninspired Thought

From time to time, the urge to dance from that place of uninhibited freedom would always tug at me to "come out and play." Each time I thought I could break away from the memory of that night by jumping back into that fast, pulsating rhythm to dance, my father's voice rushed to the forefront of my mind. It paralyzed any hint of spontaneity. I stopped doing anything creative. Dancing, pretending, make-believe, and all conversations with my imaginary friends simply ceased.

That was when I stopped listening to the creative urge inside my own heart. I began doing things that gained meapproval in the eyes of others. And, because the Universal creative impulse always corresponds to your beliefs, during that particular time my family members seemed to have agreed that they knew exactly how my life should be unfolding. It felt like they had put me on some kind of career and development plan without telling me. Over the next few years, my relatives began accumulating all the data they needed in order to write *Charles Holt's Guide to Living*.

"He's going to be a doctor," my mother said.

"No, he is going to be a preacher," said Granny, who imagined me behind a pulpit from the day I uttered my first word.

Even my uncle had his perfect plan of success for my life: "He can really hit that baseball. I believe he's going to be a famous baseball player and make lots of money."

I thought that to continue receiving attention, I would have to acquiesce to the wishes of my family and my community. Their loud and chattering voices, however well intentioned, began to drown out my own quietly unfolding dreams. Oddly enough, trying to please everybody was never painful at all; in fact, after a while, I became unconscious to why I was doing it. In order to please everybody, I grew up doing whatever they thought I should do. I mastered being the "good little boy" that everybody expected me to be. This behavior would eventually spill over into my relationships with my friends, my teachers, and my coaches. I got so good at being what other people wanted me to be that I completely forgot there was ever a time that I'd had a very deep and wonderful connection to all the things that I wanted me to be.

If this scenario sounds familiar, don't worry. You're not alone.

Many people have learned how to get by doing what is expected of them, just like I did. They don't believe, or have forgotten, that there's a possibility for greatness in their lives, independent of the fears, hopes, and dreams of family and friends. Somewhere in their past are failed attempts and dormant ideas. Though they may have learned how to get along, they've forgotten how to live.

The yearning to unlock our talents, gifts, and desires doesn't come to us for naught. These messengers are our creative bridge to the infinite—the unspeakable beauty and genius that is alive (though so often latent) in each of us. In this life, we're forever bumping into brilliance. We're forever bumping into things that have the potential to allow us to see that we're brilliant, too. But you'll never see it if you don't know what to look for, or that you should even be looking at all.

At a certain time every year, the tree that I'm sitting under blooms with the most beautiful purple flowers. Most people will pass this tree by with hardly a glance. Still others will look at it and say, "My, how pretty." But a few people will pass by this tree and hear its voice, the voice of synchronicity and perfect order, say to them, "Hmmm…you think I'm pretty? So are you. You think I smell good? So do you. You think I bloom in my season—so do you!"

When thoughts come into your awareness that show you the truth of who you are and how you fit into the world around you, I call that inspired thought. Inspired thought comes without thinking, when you stop (whether from frustration or fatigue or genuine surrender) trying so hard to figure things out. As you relax, you create an open space within that allows the intuitive awareness to be seen, heard, and felt. Inspired thought comes in a flash—generating energy and enthusiasm and an undeniable urging toward full, authentic expression. You're compelled to act. And when you act from a space of inspiration, not only are you doing something that makes you feel good about yourself, you're doing something that will ultimately make everyone feel the same goodness.

When you open up your perception, you begin to understand that life is transmitting you messages at all times. Rather than being immersed in the all-too-human quagmire of confusion, lethargy, anger, or insecurity, it becomes clear that life is working diligently to help us tap back into the flow of wholeness and well-being from which we all originally emerged.

People sometimes ask how to know whether life is sending them a message through inspired thought—or if they're simply telling themselves what they want to hear. That's a good question. Sometimes I'm not able to know right away. But then the message or awareness keeps coming back. I find myself noticing it again and again. Someone might unknowingly say or do something that brings the message to the forefront of my attention. Sometimes, even something as simple as how the lines on a tree's bark come together in a certain shape, will serve as a reminder. When life is trying to tell you something, no matter how hard you try, you just can't get away from it.

Sometimes the messages that you receive are only meant to plant a seed in the moment that you receive them. In those cases, you may have an insight but have no idea what to do with it. When faced with that kind of circumstance, it can be helpful to simply acknowledge, "I hear what's being spoken to me right now. I don't know what it means now but I'll understand it better by and by." Acknowledgment can help release the need to force an answer, thereby allowing the planted seed room to grow.

These kinds of spiritual seeds are planted in our experience all the time. They help us look at life from a larger perspective. If I'm broke and I dig around in all my pockets and I only come up with 50 cents, I can say to myself, "Oh my God, what am I going to do? I don't have any money. I can't believe this is happening to me again. There must be something wrong with me. Will I ever be able to make any real money? Other people do it. Why not me? Oh God, I can't take this anymore . . ." That's a very normal human reaction. However, if you are looking at yourself and your situation from an inspired perspective, you might find 50 cents in your pocket and say something like, "Hmmm ... I have half of a dollar. Well, thank God for that—50 cents will buy me something. I'm going to hold on to this money ..."

You've planted a seed by activating an entirely different vibration, which allows you to access the space of gratitude for having 50 cents in your pocket. This attitude is the open space for receiving and it's found in the act of being thankful for what you have now—even if you think what you have now is nothing. In the nothingness, that which you desire is created.

If you allow yourself to fall into a frantic state when unwanted happenings occur in your life, you block the lessons and the greater good that's seeking to emerge through you and the situation at hand. The inspired thought is drowned out. The seed can't find fertile ground. Nothing meaningful can come through because the mind is in total chaos. Your mental garbage is being spewed in every direction. But when you release and say, "Okay, I'm here. And I'm so glad to be here," then that which is seeking to come in and transform your way of thinking forever sees the avenue for that transformation available. It comes in and says, "Okay… you're open. Listen. Go that way. You've been set up." The Universe, like no one or nothing else, can set you up for the most wonderful things.

Chapter 2

The Seed of Conscious Choice

Embracing Conscious Creativity Over Clutter

W hatever path you choose, the state of consciousness that you're in when you choose it determines the outcome. If you allow yourself to be overtaken by uninspired thought, no matter how much you may want change or growth or positive outcomes, you will continue to be confronted by circumstances that are most closely aligned with your true state of being. If your mind is inundated with mental clutter, you'll continue to experience various forms of chaos in your life. In other words, if you walk around with the subjective belief that you've been robbed or that things have been taken from you and that things will always be taken from you, then you know what? Things will always be taken from you. Or so you'll think.

But when we embrace the power of conscious creativity, it allows the space for a different kind of choice to be made. Now, when faced with chaos or confusion or loss, we have the ability to release the chattering voices. In place of these reactive emotions, we can choose to listen to the inspired creative voice within, which says, "You know what? I've just lost this thing (or job or person) that I thought was so important to me. But I'm still here. And I'm going to be all right. As a matter of fact, I'm all right, right now. The pain that I feel is all right. The grief and the fear that I feel are all right. I recognize these feelings and choose to honor them without holding on to them or creating a story of victimhood around them. I choose not be overwhelmed with the chatter of mental garbage. I'm open to seeing where this goes."

Our ancestors knew that so well. As an African American man, my ancestors lived in a time and place where things most often didn't seem right, righteous, in order, or in line with a higher purpose. But for the most part, they knew somewhere inside that life would be all right. I know that from growing up at my grandmother's feet and from listening to the spirituals they sang and hearing the stories of the people that came before me. Those people held on to the truth that there was more to life than what they could perceive with their senses at any given moment. That's the reason they never gave up. That's the reason why I'm here—I am their answered prayer, if nothing else.

They heard the voice, just like I do, and if they heard it all those many years ago, then that says to me that the voice has never begun and will never end. The voice is everywhere—broadcasting from one Source—always leading us toward our highest good. That's why I call it the voice that matters.

When you access the voice that's derived from your Source, it allows you to remain steadfast in your awareness of universal truth—regardless of circumstances—while helping others to do the same. We need these kinds of intercessors now more then ever. Human beings have always experienced scarcity, chaos, war, unrest, and fear. But now, with 24-hour access to news feeds that barrage us with negativity everywhere we turn, the level of trepidation that individuals are experiencing in their daily lives seems to be at an all-time high. People are inundated with mental garbage—theirs and everybody else's.

It's as if everybody is looking over their shoulder, doubting the "other," who's all around them. But when you doubt somebody else, all you're saying is that you doubt yourself. When you're sure of yourself, you become aware that there's nothing that can harm you—and by "you" I mean the indestructible reality of who you are. The bottom line is that you're not going to leave the planet until you're finished doing what you came here to do. However, if you listen to the traditional media outlets, the advertising giants, and even some parts of the government, you'll hear a consistent use of scare tactics, reiterating points of view that make us feel like we need to protect the things that we think we own—or else someone will come and take them from us. Garbage chatter like this drowns out the voice that's trying to lead us toward our natural state of wholeness and grace.

Living under these circumstances, it's very easy to go into a shell and become a spiritual and emotional recluse. We take all our gifts and fold them up with the tents and put them in storage. There's a sense of isolation in modern society that breeds fear. Fear breeds hatred. Fear and hatred are kin to one another. When you fear something long enough, you begin to hate it, especially if it persists. When you find yourself thinking, *I wish they would go away (whoever "they" are),* you run into them at every corner. They're in the store. They're in the line at the bank. You see them on television, speaking eloquently and intelligently.

You want them to go away, but they won't. They can be actual people, or they can be your problems. You hate your problems but they won't go away because they've come to facilitate the next step in your evolution.

But even if you've experienced this kind of dynamic in the past, you can make a conscious choice to be different today. Living a fully actualized life is about making choices and accepting 100% responsibility not only for your actions, but for your words, thoughts, and beliefs. Each of us is completely responsible for every aspect of our lives.

I speak to a lot of young men and women in prison. Many times they say, "I don't want to be in here, and I don't deserve to be in here." These are things that they may feel adamantly about. But the way out of any prison is to go within one's self. You go inside and say, "You know what? I'm in here ('here' can be a literal prison or a situation that feels like a prison), and I'm going to take responsibility for what I did and not blame anybody else." I'm letting the blame go and saying, "I'm here right now and what can I do with this situation? What can I do for other people that may have the same issues?" That way, it's not about you any longer. You then begin to develop the facility to use your life lesson in service of someone else.

At that point, you can choose whether you want to be in prison or not. If you're ready, you can transform your life by saying, "I'm here on time. I'm here for a purpose. I don't know what it is, but I'm ready to activate a change in my life." You've now stepped out into deeper water, into a place of surrender. Once you declare that you don't know how it's going to work, but you're going to step out anyway, the Universe says, "Aha!

No more thinking on your part. You let me handle all the details because I have all the answers. And through me, so do you." But you have to consciously choose to silence the chatter and release the garbage that the chattering voices heap onto your mind before it's possible to fully step into surrender.

When you're filled with the chaos of mental garbage, outside influences have a much easier time playing on your psyche. You don't know about tomorrow, the chatter tells you. "Collect your things, everything you can, and head for the hills! Because you just don't know!" You can believe in that perspective. Or you can make another choice to release that kind of frantic chatter and say, "Things are things. They come and they go. I want to contribute to the creation of what is unfolding on the planet. That's what I stand for. Nothing, and no one, can take that away from me."

This is an extremely important practice to cultivate. If we allow mental garbage to cloud our awareness, our ability to hear the voice within gets drowned out. We feel lost in the world, unsure of ourselves and vaguely uneasy about whether we're good enough to compete in our constantly shifting, high-tech society. We feel a lack of purpose. That's how I felt for many years, having let go of my heart's desire and saddling myself instead with all of the "supposed to be's" of the people around me.

Conversely, through the moment-by-moment cultivation of conscious choice, one becomes keenly aware of the seed within. Buried inside this seed is the understanding of our oneness with the voice of unconditional love. The voice arising from that seed continues to say, "This beauty, this unconditional love, this joy, this abundance is the truth of who you are." It doesn't matter what's going on around you, what your own mental garbage is telling you, or what people have said and done to you. Surrendering to this voice leaves room for inspired thought to take over and lead you anywhere you want to go. Some people call this spontaneous unfolding of goodness miraculous. It's really the natural state of our being.

The Music and the Miracles

One day, when I was 15, I experienced just such a miracle: an instantaneous revelation of the truth of my being. For me, the revelation happened through music. On that day, I'd gone to my friend Vanessa's house on Taylor Road to hang out. Vanessa greeted me at the door, then went into the living room and put on a Donny Hathaway record. I didn't know who Donny Hathaway was at the time. But when I heard the first notes of "A Song For You," something bolted awake inside me. I remember saying to myself, "One day I'm going to sing like that." I was a star athlete and a straight A student at the time. There was absolutely no indication that I would do anything creative with my life. But still, Donny Hathaway's voice connected with the voice of spirit within me, the part of me that had subconsciously held on to the awareness of my divine purpose. Although I didn't understand it for many years, something beautiful and powerful was activated within me that day.

As I listened to Hathaway, I forgot about everything. The effect his voice had on me was immediate. It was as though I was really hearing music for the first time in my life. I felt like I understood exactly what he was feeling with every note he sang. Though often full of haunting shadows, the stories he told with such conviction through his music were incredibly vivid. They were filled with rich, dusty orange tones like the last moments of sun before it melts behind a mountain range. I was so moved that I went out and purchased every Donny Hathaway cassette I could find.

I listened to his music hours upon hours. I couldn't have explained to anybody what this passion for music was, but I knew that if nothing else, this was music that I needed to listen to. I needed to hear it. It seemed like he was singing the tune of my life: The sharp sadness, the loneliness and the feeling of not fitting in. Even when I was in familiar environments, the nervous unsettling in my stomach seemed to overshadow the happiness. I couldn't explain the feeling to anyone. I didn't understand it myself. The only thing I could relate it to was the feeling of being left in the dust during an innocent footrace with my older brother in our backyard. For some reason I always felt I was being left behind, like I was always trying to catch up to that elusive something in my life.

In hindsight, I understand that such feelings and insecurities occur naturally when the voice of connection and self-expression has been silenced, because it's the voice that tells us why we're here on this planet at this time. When we don't listen, or don't understand what we're hearing, it's very easy to feel separated and anxious. That's when the chattering voices take off and the mental garbage begins to pile sky-high.

There may be dreams and visions that you've held hostage since childhood. For whatever reason, you may have had the impulse to dream beaten out of you by experience. You may have thrown away those moments of spontaneous brilliance as void, thinking they'd go away forever. I'm here to tell you that they won't. They are as near to you as the very air you breathe. Rather than assuming that the spark will eventually die out, or has already died out, know that the real process revolves around releasing the layers of debris that have smothered its glow.

Close your eyes and imagine yourself as an onion. Start peeling back the layers. At the center of the onion is a little pearl that contains everything that you need to fulfill whatever it is that you've been called to do on this planet. The layers represent all the lies that you've somehow learned over the course of your lifetime, the garbage voices that masquerade as your thoughts:

You can't do it.

You're going to be a nobody.

You failed at school and you'll probably fail at everything else...

You're a black man in a white man's world.

You're a woman in a man's world.

You're not smart enough.

You're not pretty/handsome enough.

Conversely, if you're like me, you've grown into adulthood feeling suffocated by the mountainous expectations of others (parents in particular). The people closest to you in your life may have bombarded you with a well-meaning swarm of backhanded praise:

"I know you can do it—just try harder."

"You are the best!"

"I expect nothing but greatness from you...I know you won't let me down."

For most people, the list goes on and on. When you begin to deliberately peel back the layers, you find yourself accessing parts of your real nature that have been hidden for years, sometimes for your entire life.

When a person releases the false voices, even if only for a second, and experiences the revelation of the authentic nature of his or her being, it's nothing short of miraculous. We often stumble through life trying to force miracles, when there are miracles happening around us all the time. That energy never goes away. It's the energy that says you can do and be anything that you want to because you're brilliant! (And not from a place of expectation or anticipation, but from a space of loving acceptance grounded in spiritual principle). But we have to peel back the layers to get to it. Some layers are harder to peel back than others. Some layers, when we peel them back, squirt in our eyes and make us cry. There are often the greatest lessons in those layers.

We Are All Someone's Answered Prayer

The lessons of our experience don't come just for us. They come for others as well. When we become trapped beneath the mental garbage that tells us that our problem or circumstance is so much worse than everybody else's, that's a form of separation. We separate ourselves from others and we separate ourselves from the miracle of our own transformation, as it seeks to emerge from the trials that provide our greatest lessons. No matter what you've been through, there's a lesson in it.

For example, slavery was horrible, but there was a lesson in it. One of the lessons for my ancestors was to pray and live in a way that prevented their descendants from going through the emotional and physical degradation of what they went through. They learned to pray, believing that their descendants would be doctors and teachers, that they would have an effective and transformative voice in the world and be able to read and write books, that they could be world leaders and presidents. That was a lesson in faith for my ancestors, which means that African Americans today are answered prayers, the next step in the evolution of a people in an ever-expanding universe.

So what are we praying for? What will generations after us become because of what we've created here now? Are we content to believe in the garbage that seeks to keep us trapped in mediocrity and inefficiency and pain? Or are we looking toward something greater? Be assured that in this process of conscious creation, there will be trials. You're going to have dark nights of the soul, because they're necessary. Those dark nights squeeze us because something wants to emerge. The lesson within the emergence causes us to pause. It may cause us to meditate and, in our meditation, it becomes possible to get what we're here for.

Achieving this level of understanding, while releasing the layers of mental garbage that have so far prevented us from getting there, also requires us to live a blame-free life. With the conscious choice to live blame-free comes the opportunity to forgive. Once we agree that there's nothing to blame anybody about or for, we realize that all the stuff we hold people in mental and emotional bondage over is silly. From that point of view, forgiveness becomes sacred. Conversely, holding on to blame and unforgiveness becomes just too costly. It clouds the mind and heart, often causing us to lash out against others, whether they've done anything to warrant the behavior or not.

Once I realized that, I understood that people were not out to get me as I'd once believed. People weren't waiting for me to walk into a store and steal something, because I don't steal. People don't think I'm an angry black man, because I'm not an angry black man.

So why were those thoughts in my mind?

Those thoughts were in my mind for the same reason that we all hold false thoughts and beliefs about ourselves and the world around us: It's the ego talking. The egoic mind is the place where our mental garbage is created and stored. The chatter of the ego will always try to drown out the voice of Source within.

The voice tells you that you're a wondrous manifestation of unconditional love. The chatter of the ego tells you that there's something wrong with you and you need to fix it—quick before anybody else finds out! We must begin to trust ourselves. We must trust that who we are is okay and what we are doing is okay. We must trust that our lives are okay. Challenging the toxic voice of the ego may sound something like this:

"Even though my family said that I was goin' to hell because I had a baby out of wedlock, I'm still okay."

"Even if I didn't follow the path that my parents had planned for me, I am okay."

"Even if the preacher said that homosexuals were going to burn in a lake of fire, I'm okay."

Being able to claim the truth of who you are in a spirit of loving compassion is crucial to living a fully expressed life. There will always be individuals who'll judge or criticize those whom they deem different or unacceptable. We see this everyday in the world around us. We condemn each other for being the wrong race, the wrong age, the wrong socio-economic class, or loving someone of the wrong gender. This is ridiculous!

When people are trying to come to terms with who they are, particularly when sorting out something as intimate as their sexual preference, they need to be showered with love and compassion rather than judgment and shame. In these cases, we must find (or become) part of a strong support system. Surround yourself with other voices whose presence can help drown out the loud voices of judgment and intolerance. Find a mentor whose self-expression is vibrant. Then ask yourself the question: is it possible for me to live my life like this, to come to grips with the fact that I'm okay just the way I am?

No matter what your issue may be, you have the right to be yourself, fully expressed.

Things and people will come to try to keep you small. Sometimes, they'll take the worst things you've ever done in your life and try to throw them back in your face. But when they say, "I see you were in a correctional facility" you can say without shame, "Yes, ma'am, I was in a correctional facility." Or, "Yes, sir, I was doing drugs. But I found myself while I was there, and I'm all right now."

You don't have to hold your head down and worry about what "they" are going to think about you. The question is: What do you think about you? What has the voice told you about who you are? If you don't know, the rest of the world will gladly tell you who you are. And most likely, whatever the world says will be nothing close to the truth.

We must be willing to step out of the falsehoods of "the way things are" and "the way I am" and "the way I'll always be." These static attitudes and beliefs usually bring with them great pain and sadness. We must be willing to let these go, stepping into the unknown and making life welcome. When you're in a state of openness and gratitude, you're actually welcoming the goodness that wants to come your way. If you choose to be closed or unwilling, things may still come to you. But the consciousness may not be open enough to receive the lesson. Remember, there's always a lesson, whether it looks good or looks bad. But being in a state of thankfulness allows your consciousness to say, "Okay, there was a lesson in this, rather than saying, I don't care. I don't want to hear the lesson. This didn't work out the way I wanted it to!"

Being able to see the value in your lessons is directly related to cultivating the ability to always seek the good, in yourself and in others, and learning to consistently hear the voice of truth.

Exercise

Quite often, our mental garbage revolves around thoughts of not being enough. You may secretly feel that you're not good enough, not rich enough, not worthy of love and support, not smart enough, etc. It may seem that everyone else's life is moving forward at a brisk and exciting pace, while yours is at a standstill—or worse, going backwards. It can be very hard to seriously imagine living a fabulous life where you have everything that you want and have worked for. Whether what you crave is money, love, fame, or freedom, it can be a frightening prospect to really entertain what your life would be like if you actually received all you desired. After all, if life were that wonderful, what would the chattering voices have to complain about?

Someone once invited me to take part in a profound exercise, and now I invite you to engage in it as well.

Imagine that someone hands you a million-dollar bill. It's real, and it's all yours. Imagine all the things you're going to buy and do with that money. See it all—feel it, relish it. Really take in what it's like to have everything you've ever wanted. Then ask yourself the question:

So what are you going to do now?

When I was given that fake million-dollar bill, I suddenly became child-like and began letting my imagination roam. I pictured relaxing in the entertainment room of my dream house with my choice of favorite car parked in the garage. I saw myself taking a leisurely, romantic stroll on the shores of the Mediterranean on a long, exotic vacation. My bank account sported a hefty, upward six-figure number with promising prospects for increase. I meditated on this feeling for nearly ten minutes. *Good, golly,* I thought. *I'll never have to worry about finances again! I have everything I've ever dreamed of.* As I sank deeper in this present "create-my-life" fantasy world, an inquiring voice quickly surfaced. "Okay," it said. "So now I have it all, what's next?"

With that thought, it felt like a rock had landed in the pit of my stomach. I said, "Oh my God. I'm not doing anything with my life ... or for anybody else's!"

And the voice answered, "There it is! The missing ingredient. That's the reason why you're here. We're all here for somebody else's good."

Most people make the mistake of thinking life is all about attaining material good, or whatever they equate with "perfection" and "having it all." Then they wonder why the "perfection" continues to elude them. Or, if they finally get what they thought they wanted, they wonder why they continue to feel unfulfilled. This happens when people are seduced by the idea of having an ideal life without thinking deeply about what actually creates sustainable happiness.

The answer to that conundrum is the same answer that will silence the chattering voices: Dedicating yourself to giving meaningfully to others.

Because even if you had everything you desire, you'd still have to fill your days, and your heart, with something more. If you miss this crucial step, you miss the opportunity to step out of yourself, to step away from the ego with its chattering, fearful, selfish, and self-involved voices, and into something greater.

You can do this exercise by imagining yourself in possession of anything that you feel is lacking in your life. What would it be like to be joyously married to your soul mate? How would it feel to step out on stage and act? What would it feel like to be unconditionally loved by all the people in your life, without being bound by anger, fear, or guilt? How would it be to experience that level of total freedom?

After you ask what your good looks like and feels like, it's time for the most important question of all: How does the good that I experience benefit the world around me?

Once you begin to grasp the understanding of what it's like to live this kind of existence, it becomes easier to imagine a healthy, happy, and whole life, without the chattering voices of failure and fear seeking to block you at every turn. This is where real freedom and joy become not just possibilities, but mandates.

Chapter 3

Learning How to Listen Again

Rediscovering the Connection

C hildren are born connected to the voice of internal wisdom.

As a child, I had a wonderful connection to that animating voice, which spoke directly to the joy inherent inside my soul. I could see and feel it all around me. Like all children, I lived fully in the moment. I wasn't attached to anything. When people said things about me that might have sounded judgmental or unkind, those words simply didn't stick in my awareness.

Disapproving statements didn't have an impact on me until I began to hear those things from the people in my life that I considered authority figures: Specifically my parents and siblings. I often heard statements like, "You can't do that" or "That doesn't fit you" or "You're a boy ... you're not supposed to be dancing and tumbling!" Over time, these reprimands took on a new meaning and consequence that was in direct contradiction to the joyous voice within me that said, "Hey! Let's go have fun! Let's go outside and turn flips!"

After repeatedly being told that something was wrong with my behavior, like so many children, I began to believe that the real meaning behind that reproach was: Something is wrong with me.

When we start thinking that we're wrong or less than for being who we are, or that we don't necessarily fit in, it's easy to become spiritually and emotionally reclusive. So even when the joyous voice within you says, "Let's go out and play," very often the response that comes up is, "No. I can't do that."

This is where the voices of doubt and fear and worry begin to creep into our lives, sidelining us from participating and living full out. As we grow older, those ways of thinking become ways of being, which begin to cement. Suddenly, we're not sure if we fit in. We don't know if we're good enough the way that we are. Not only will such thoughts stop us from being active participants in the lives of others, but they can also stop us from actively participating in our own lives.

Sometimes this pattern of self-doubt can build up over time. Or it might be initiated by a single word, incident, or action that takes root inside an impressionable mind. Maybe you messed up during a piano recital and had the thought, *Oh, I wasn't good enough.* Slowly, music began to lose its appeal for you and eventually you stopped playing the piano all together. No matter whether the trigger was big or small, whether it was one incident or a series of failures, the result is the same: The growth of distrust in your innate wisdom and uniqueness.

Children come to this planet with the desire to participate fully in all that life has to offer. When children are allowed to just be, when they're not restrained, they give 100 percent of who and what they are to life. But if the children repeatedly hear judgmental, confining, or belittling words, they begin to form their self-concept around those words.

A parent says, "Don't ever do that again! You're so silly!"

The child internalizes: I'm silly. I can't ever do that again or everyone will know I'm there's something wrong with me.

But the intuitive nature of children says, "Yeah! Let's have fun! I'll never look stupid because I'm not stupid! I'll never look silly because I'm not silly! I'll never say anything dumb because I'm not dumb and I don't say dumb things!" That's the space that kids live from, until somebody tells them otherwise.

The natural mind of a child is free. When you're free in your mind, everything else follows suit. You're free in your body; you dance like you want to dance. You're free in your heart; you love fully, without reservation. Likewise, you create from this space of freedom. If you are entangled in your head, then you'll be entangled in any endeavor that you choose to take on.

For example, my heart may tell me, "Start your own garden, and then you can teach other people how to garden. It's something that you've loved to do all your life, and now you have an opportunity to do it."

But then my head will jump in and say, "But I can't make any money gardening. And I need to make money."

Those who have reconnected with their internal wisdom are able to say, "You know what? I'm going back to gardening. Money can't satisfy me. It can't create this happiness within me. Gardening does that. I trust that if I'm called to do this, I'll be supported every step of the way—including financially!"

We finally find that we're following the path of the intuitive.

Some of us find it sooner rather than later. But the child is always aware of that path. The child within is always looking for ways to express because they live in a world of possibility.

Resilience

Some people hear disparaging words from others and are crushed by these words, totally disconnecting to the truth of their authentic self. However, some people can repel the harmful words of others. They maintain their natural resilience and a very keen sense of who they are as spiritual beings. We all have the ability to access this type of resilience. We all have a holy mandate to fulfill here on this planet. Some of us get connected to our holy mandate from an internal knowing or through the words of others. In times of hardship, the conviction and guiding words come forth to lead us through the trials.

One of the biggest problems that arise is when individuals are not passionate enough about the mandate to step out into the deep. It takes a leap of faith to believe that one is going to be supported even when the way is not clearly shown. When one cannot make that leap, it becomes easier to put one's head down and hope that the calling and the desire will pass. But it won't. Whatever our own personal "it" is, the fulfillment of "it" is the reason why we've come to this planet.

Recognizing When and Where We Stopped Listening

Shortly after the incident in which my father scolded me for "performing in front of grown folks" and being "in grown folks business," everything became a push for me. When we step out of our authentic self, so many aspects of life become a push, or a grind. When we're acting in the ease and grace of who we are, things flow. For me, the grind was believing that I had to do something other than perform to make the people around me happy. I didn't want my parents to think badly of me. I didn't want the other kids to make fun of me or call me names like "sissy" because I liked to tumble and dance. So, I thought to myself, *I should play baseball! I like playing baseball anyway.*

When you're true to your authentic self, you're enthusiastic about life and everything around you begins to activate at that vibration. When you try to do what others think is more appropriate, life begins to drain of its color and vibrancy. The energy stops flowing. That's when the pushing begins.

When I was five years old, I tried to push my way into being accepted. I started playing sports. As luck would have it, I happened to be a great athlete. Athletics began to fold over my previous desires and I let it happen willingly, because I wanted to acquiesce to what everyone else thought I should be.

Be more of a little Southern boy. Be more of a little Southern Christian boy. Be more of a little Southern Christian black boy.

The litany continued to grow longer and longer the older I became. "Charles" became buried under a mountain of cultural codes that signaled who and what he should be at any given moment. I began to think in terms of, *How am I going to look to them?* Everything shifted.

When you begin to consciously or unconsciously change who you are to suit the preferences of others, it allows the insidious thought forms that tell you that you're not enough to enter into your awareness. You have to do something extra, push harder, to be enough. You have to be somebody else to really be liked and be impressive to others. And so you create yourself anew. This "not enough" consciousness initiates a cycle, which encourages people to live out their lives playing roles that were never meant to fit them.

Once started, this cycle will continue unabated until something inside wakes up and says, "I don't give a damn what they think about me anymore! I am going to be me. I was joyful as a child, before I bought into what everyone else said should make me happy, and I can be happy like that again. I may have to leave where I am. I may have to strike out on my own to find that feeling again, to peel back the layers. But I know it's there, because I've had it before and I can have it again."

It's important, if possible, to be able to articulate when and where in your life you stopped listening to your authentic voice. If you don't remember or don't know how to verbally articulate what may have caused the disconnection to occur for you, take some time to sit in the silence and breathe. As you allow yourself to be more open, the insights will burst forth.

I remember a workshop I conducted called "Finding Your Voice," in which one of the participants had a particularly memorable breakthrough. The young lady's name was Ann, and I noticed her right away because she had a deep resistance to smiling. Rather than allowing a full smile to cross her face, Ann would press her lips together in a "Grinch-who-stole-Christmas" grin. I thought, *How interesting. This young woman is sitting in a workshop dedicated to finding your voice, and she can't even open her mouth.*

We went around the room telling a little about ourselves. When it was Ann's turn, she told everyone that she'd just been accepted to law school. This was wonderful news and everyone in the room was impressed, but she said it with her head down.

I said, "Wait a minute. You just got accepted into law school?"

"Yeah," she replied, with her head still down. "Can you believe it?"

Body posture says what language is rarely able to articulate. As I watched this young woman share, I thought, *Oh, so they've accepted you, but you haven't accepted yourself!*

We continued on and got further into the real work that we'd come there to do. The workshop was extraordinary. We had breakdowns and breakthroughs. At certain a point, I asked a question and no one wanted to answer.

"If no one answers," I told the 50 or so participants sitting around the room, "I'm going to start calling on people."

Again, I noticed Ann put her head down, as though she were trying to hide. So I purposely called on her and said, "You, come on up here!"

Ann looked like she saw a ghost. Her eyes bulged out. Her body became rigid and stiff.

"Me?" she squeaked.

"Yes, you," I replied. "Come on."

She got in the middle of our circle and we began to talk.

I said, "This whole process has been about finding your

voice. There are many singers and musicians who are here today because they want to take their craft to the next level. But the things that we've been talking about today are for anyone who is involved in transforming themselves and moving to the next plateau in their unfolding. So, tell me about music in your life, because music is a universal tuning fork, so to speak. Do you remember any songs that were sung to you when you were younger? If so, which one stood out?"

"Yes," Ann said. "I remember a song that my fourth grade teacher sang to me."

Normally, when people remember songs they remember songs that were sung to them by their parents or grandparents. These are the songs that generally make the strongest impression. So I immediately picked up that there must have been some kind of strong energy that this woman's fourth grade teacher exposed her to.

I said, "Please, sing a little bit of the song."

"I don't remember it," she responded.

"Oh, yes you do," I countered.

"I'm not a singer," she said.

"Oh, yes you are," I told her. "There's a song in you. There's a song in everybody."

This young woman began to sing.

"I ... can ... do ... anything ... I ... want ... to ... do ..."

The words came out in a small, choppy voice. Suddenly Ann broke down into tears.

"Why are you crying?" I asked.

"Because," she said, "I've never really felt that way."

I admonished her to continue.

Ann started the next verse of the song, and a flood of tears began pouring down her face.

"I want you to hold your head up," I told her. "And I want you to sing like the words say: I can do anything I want to! Know that when you're saying this, you're not saying it out of pride, you're saying it out of recognition."

Once again, the young woman began to sing.

All of a sudden, she screamed out, "I forgive you, Mommy!"

At that time I knew—and she did, too—that she'd allowed the things that she'd been told as a child to hold her hostage. Not only that, but she'd held her mother hostage for saying the words that had so wounded her.

Lost in this decades-old emotional release, the woman continued on, crying out, "I forgive you for telling me I was going to be a nobody! I forgive you for telling me that I was ugly... that I was too black!"

So often, people hide this kind of deep, primal pain even from themselves because they don't feel capable of dealing with it. But the authentic voice, the voice that matters, is right there saying, "Yes! Let's get it all out. I'm ready! Let's get it all out so we can move on. I can release you and release myself at the same time."

Once she'd calmed down, Ann admitted in front of the whole class, "Yes, my mother said all those things to me."

I told her, "Look, you're about to embark on the first leg of your journey toward becoming a judge. You have to be able to stand fully in your power to be able to command that kind of authority. You've got to be able to look at yourself every day in the mirror and say, 'Yes! I am enough!'"

If You Stopped Listening,
How Do You Start Listening Again?

Do you recognize yourself in any of this? If you feel that somewhere along the way you may have lost touch with your voice, your authentic self, by allowing yourself to be made over into a more appropriate, acceptable image, you can start finding your way back to truth by asking some simple questions.

Start off with this one: Am I truly happy with the way my life is in this moment?

Now, it's possible to try to trick yourself by saying, "Yeah, I'm happy. I have a nice home. I have a nice family. My wife/husband/significant other is great. I have great children. I have a great job ..." And then something will speak and ask you, "Are you really happy though? Are you really living the life that you love and were called to live?"

There's a place in truth that defies all fact or statistic. Facts and statistics tell you that people with a level of education comparable to yours make a certain amount of money, live in certain neighborhoods, etc. The facts of a situation will tell you that, because you have all the trappings of success, then therefore you must be happy. Conversely, if you don't have these things, then of course you must be miserable and disgruntled.

But beyond what the facts may say about you, there's the truth of who you are. When you ask yourself questions like, "Am I happy?" you give your truth a voice. Truth isn't concerned with facts or statistics. Truth is concerned with truth.

Am I happy? Am I fulfilled? Am I where I want to be?

Your honest answers to these questions will begin to tell you whether or not you've strayed far from your authentic self and the voice that matters within you. If you have, as you answer these questions, the answers will help you begin to pinpoint where the paths in your life diverged. For example, if you realize that you're not happy in your career, you can continue by questioning yourself about why you stopped doing the things that you absolutely loved to do. If you stopped, when did you stop? What made you believe what you love to do could not also be turned into a fulfilling and lucrative career? Who or what first told you that that would be impossible?

What if all the things that I've accumulated over the years suddenly disappeared? Would I look at my life and still consider myself happy?

In the process of re-learning how to listen and peeling back the layers, you can also ask yourself questions like: "Why am I here?" "What is my true purpose for being here on this planet at this time?" "Who am I?" "Am I what someone else said about me?" or "What have others said about me that I've started to become?"

Meditate on these questions, and slowly allow the answers to well up from deep within the center of your being. Be silent. Allow the voice that matters to speak into that silence. However, you should be aware that the other voices, the ego voices, will also try to speak into that silence.

"What do you mean you want to be a novelist? That's never going to happen! You're never going to get out of the dead-end job that you already have because you're not good at anything else! That's what your momma said. You're daddy was the same way, too. He was full of pipe dreams, but never amounted to anything. So it's all right. Just accept that the apple can't fall too far from the tree. That's just the way you are."

When such voices pry their way into your awareness, continue to ask mindful questions. "Am I really just a dreamer? Is there more to me than that? Who was I before I started identifying myself that way?"

The egoic, chattering voices are very quick to justify all the things that we do to keep ourselves off the path toward self-actualization and fulfillment. Tuning in to your authentic voice breaks down these justifications and requires you to get real with yourself.

Quite often, people ask questions like the ones previously mentioned in a kind of glib or halfhearted way. They don't really look for the manifestation of what they've requested. So when answers come to them, showing them why they're here or who they are behind the carefully placed mask, they don't even realize it. We may feel like we're stuck in a rut and pray to God for a shift in our lives, but then we don't look for the shift. We don't set the intention to be aware of the shift when it occurs and then stay diligently focused until we see it manifest.

We ask for a major change in our lives and then, six months later, we say, "Oh God! Why does it feel like everything is crumbling around me? I don't understand!" What is there not to understand? The change that was requested has occurred. But we feel pain because we're still trying to hold on to that which we claimed we didn't want anymore.

Listen. Meditate. Remember. In the silence that arises, you'll hear the voice of your Source telling you, "Be still. You asked for this, remember?"

Are You Ready for a Breakthrough?

I believe that we are, to a very meaningful extent, products of our environment. When I was ready for a breakthrough, one of the things that I knew I'd have to do was remove myself from the environment that caused me to view life as static and predictable. If you find yourself in any kind of environment where negativity or fear hold sway, it may be time to physically remove yourself.

Conversely, sometimes the nest is too comfortable. Sometimes, the people around us are totally loving and encouraging and supportive. But unless and until you believe the same truths about yourself that your parents and others seem to see, you'll never be able to fully actualize or embody their vision of you. Until you get out and apply yourself in an environment where you can test the proverbial waters on your own, a shadow of doubt will remain hovering over you.

As the Bible says, "Show yourself approved." When you're ready for a breakthrough in your life, it means that you're ready to put into practice that which you say that you know. This is the start of your journey in peeling back the layers that have heretofore obscured your view of the beauty and power of your genuine self. As you peel back these layers, you find out what your subconscious beliefs really are about yourself and how these beliefs have been operating, sometimes completely unchallenged, as laws in your life. No matter how painful these revelations may be, know that they are really spiritual gems strewn along the path of this journey to help guide you to your greatest heights.

However, because these revelations tend to show up in our lives looking like anything but precious treasures, it can be very disheartening and downright confusing when you're confronted with their appearance. Quite often, breakthroughs are heralded by the appearance of failure, chaos, endings, and interrupted patterns. This process feels bad, but is actually a good thing because it means that something is shifting. When something new is trying to emerge, our mental conditioning generally tells us that our way of life—the things we're used to being, having, or doing—is being challenged. Whenever you have a challenge, it tends to be internalized as some kind of conflict, whether the conflict is in your mind, in the way you treat people, or the way you perform on your job.

On some level, we know what's going on. On a conscious level, you may say, "Oh, I'm not feeling right today" or "Something's up!" or even, "Man, I'm pissed!" Experiencing those types of emotions gives us the opportunity to ask, What's caused me to feel this way? What's really going on?

There's an integration period that occurs when one paradigm is moving out of focus and another one is moving in. When we recognize and internalize the fact that the painful part of the process is also an integral component to our growth, the possibility arises for us to be gentle and patient with ourselves. Whatever paradigm we may be experiencing, we know that there's always a platform for us to experience the other voice— the flip side of that paradigm.

We never want ourselves to be stuck in an optionless world. We always want to give ourselves the opportunity to choose something different. What we're facing today isn't the only option we have. If our option looks good, it can get even better. If it's not so good, we can choose to continue to go down that road, or we can flip the script in our minds and agree to experience something better.

We may not understand fully or be able to articulate the shift from a mental standpoint, but there's something inside that's gravitating to this new dynamic. What is unfolding is the unknown. The unknown is not a comfortable place because we don't get the opportunity to control it. But stepping into the unknown gives us the power to step out into the "promised land," as Dr. Michael Beckwith says, which is our own magnificence.

As we step further into that greatness, we can say, "I know that these uncomfortable things are coming up for me to be able to take a good look at." The intention is to get us to ask more questions of ourselves. When we stop asking questions is when we begin to experience the downward portion of the spiral regarding what life is trying to teach us—the ruts and the potholes on the path. But all life is doing is saying, "Ask me a question!"

What kinds of questions? Questions like: How did I get to this place? Why do I feel like this? How can life be better? How can I get a better job to support my family? How can I be a help to my mother? To my classmates? What can I do to promote peace on Earth? and How can I be a beneficial presence on the planet?

These are empowering, worthwhile questions. The teacher called life is trying to get us in a position where we'll ask these questions, so that the master guide inside can give us the answers.

Chapter 4

Losing Your Dreams, Gaining Yourself

My Story

Growing up, nearly all the kids in the neighborhood who participated on athletic teams were involved in contact sports like football, basketball, and boxing. Many chose the tough games to keep from being picked on or teased by those who were bigger and stronger. If you were thought to be weak, you were more likely to be the target of cruel jokes and beat downs by older kids. My brother was well respected in our community, so the last thing I had to worry about was being bothered by others. But he thought it would do me some good to join a football team so I could build toughness. According to him, I had become quite graceful and limber from practicing cartwheels in the backyard. He begged my mother to let me play football. I didn't want my brother to call me a sissy, so I went along with his wishes. Being labeled a sissy was like being cursed: No friends, no respect, and no fun. My mother was afraid that I might get hurt and didn't think football was a good idea at first, but she finally agreed to allow me to try out.

Pasquale's Pizza was my first football team. I was the last-string tailback my first year, but it only took me touching the football for the first time in a game for my coach to find out that I possessed the most dangerous weapon anybody could have on the football field: Speed. For most of the season, I'd watched each game from the sidelines with an opportunity to participate on special teams if we were beating an opponent by a lot of points. I yearned to experience the feeling of getting to carry the football in a game. However, at the same time, I despised being tackled and pounded to the ground. I was the star running back on the meat squad during practice, and even then I avoided being hit as much as possible by the defensive stalwarts on the team.

Close to the end of the season, both of our starters at running back got injured. This meant that unless the coach decided to pull a player from another position to fill the running back slot, I'd be the one called on. I was nervous being the go-to man, but I was ready. I was the fastest player on the team, and the first time I got the ball, I carried it 80 yards for a touchdown. It was called back because of a penalty, but my coach had enough faith in me to call the same exact play on the next down.

"Come on, Charlie, you can do it again," my teammates encouraged. The name he gave the play was: "Run, Charlie, Run." I remember taking the handoff, cutting off the butt of the right guard, ditching the free safety with a Heisman-like move, and running straight down the middle of the field as fast as I could, like a man possessed, with my eyes fixed on those goal posts. All my teammates ran to the end zone and picked me up in the air, chanting, "Char-lie! Char-lie! Char-lie!"

This experience created a feeling of euphoria that I lived and re-lived for months. It reminded me of my mother's words that I could achieve anything I imagined, no matter the situation or circumstance. From that day forward, I became a celebrated athlete—a star football player, sprinter, and baseball player who began seriously considering my brother's and my uncle's dreams of one day playing sports professionally.

By my junior year, playing football had taken precedence over everything. I ate, breathed, and dreamed football, often falling asleep with my helmet in my hands. I watched college football games all day Saturday and hurried home to watch professional games after church on Sunday. As I became entranced in the game, I envisioned myself one day playing on Sunday afternoons. It wasn't such a far-fetched idea. I'd already gotten interest from some of the country's top collegiate football programs, and after the season was over I began to take recruiting trips to prospective schools for weekend visits.

Most of the larger schools wanted me to sit out for a year or two to learn the system and be tutored by the older, more experienced players at my position. They thought it would provide me with valuable experience and give me a couple of years to put on a few needed pounds of muscle. In hindsight, this option would have only enhanced my chances of playing on Sunday afternoons. But I wanted to play my first year and was insistent on having things my way. In spite of all of the wise advice given by my high school coach and my brother, who wanted me to attend a school that would nurture me for a couple of years before letting me play, my ego managed to outweigh their words. I accepted a scholarship offer from one of the schools that had promised me playing time as a freshman.

I got what I so desperately wished for ... and was miserable my first two years of college. The only consolation I found during my entire time there was sitting on the brick wall outside of the Flowers Hall dormitory with my teammate and friend Roger Dukes from Mississippi, singing rhythm-and-blues songs to the girls at Rice Hall. It was the only thing that seemed to make me remotely happy. At the time, I didn't think too deeply into the reason why singing songs consoled me at one of the most difficult times in my life. My mind was fixated on sports.

I transferred schools twice, finally ending up at a small liberal arts school in Memphis where I earned a bachelors degree in sociology. Rhodes College, my alma mater, wasn't at all what I had dreamed of in terms of fulfilling a destiny to play professional football; a Division III school whose season's best was defeating conference archrival University of the South at Sewanee. However, it was the perfect place for what I had been groomed to experience with regard to academics. With a school honor code to encourage truthful expression and examination, the environment at Rhodes paralleled the integrity that I'd known growing up in my small community in Nashville. It also reflected the essence of excellence I stood for as a student and individual as well.

My college football campaign was less than stellar. During the two-week football camp in August, just a week before the opening game of my junior season, I injured my knee during an intrasquad scrimmage. I was about to turn upfield after catching a pass when the nearside defensive back, in full stride, shoved his shoulder into my left knee. The sting from the contact ran through my entire body. After the tackle, I laid on the field, grabbing my leg, fearing something horrible had happened. I tried standing up, but I was in too much pain and I fell back to the ground. Too prideful to allow my teammates help me to the sideline, I managed to hobble off of the field on one leg and to the training room. By the time I arrived, my knee was the size of a grapefruit. This was a devastating blow for me. I'd never experienced a serious injury. In fact, I'd only missed one game in my entire athletic career, and that was because my mother stood in front of my bedroom door insisting I couldn't play with the flu.

The knee injury sidelined me for the entire season. Determined that I'd return for my senior campaign, Brian, the school's physical trainer, and I spent eight months of intense workouts and rehab. In one of the training rooms, there was a wilted picture taped up against the drab, gray wall of a climber scaling to the top of a mountain. The word "perseverance" was in bold print. Everyday in rehab, in that small, boxlike room, I used that picture as my inspiration and the word *perseverance* as my mantra.

By the end of the second semester, my knee was at 90 percent strength. That summer before my senior campaign, I dedicated a couple of hours a day to the speed and quickness drills I'd learned while running track. Many of my teammates assisted me in drills, which made my journey back to the football field even more special, and all the hard work and dedication paid off. I started every game, and concluded my college career with honors and as a member of the first team in the school's history to make it to postseason playoffs.

I couldn't imagine my life without football, so I continued to work out diligently after the season was over, praying that I'd get the opportunity to continue my career at the professional level. I got the opportunity to do drills and tests for several NFL scouts. After doing strength tests and drills for the Cleveland Browns, I went to see Kyle Rote, Jr., the agent who had set my appointment.

"Do you think they're going to pick me up?" I asked in optimistic tone. "You think they're going to sign me?"

"You know," he said slowly, "I don't know."

"I had a great work out for them," I persisted.

As I sat across from him, he paused, looked at me, and uttered words that ran through me like a bone-chilling wind.

"Charles, maybe you're not supposed to be playing professional football."

When he said that, something rose up in me and I snapped, "Oh, yes I am! This is what I've trained all my life for!"

Kyle just smiled at me. Clearly, he'd been through this before.

"Okay. Okay," he said. "We'll get you a team."

But we both knew that wasn't true. Whether I wanted to or not, I had to accept that no one had opted to sign me. My dreams of playing pro football were over. It was the most disappointment I'd ever experienced in my life. It felt like my heart had been ripped out of my body. In my mind, I saw no other choice for my life and future besides football. My ego was very quick to tell me that football was my life and the one true, meaningful path to fulfilling my destiny.

However, if I'd listened a little deeper, I'd have heard another voice, a more honest voice telling me that all those things that I'd chosen to believe simply weren't true.

Listening to the voice within allows people to know that

there's always another choice. It doesn't matter whether you're talking about big life choices like which career path to follow or the moment-by-moment decisions that we all make every day while sitting at a traffic light or walking down the stairs, which also affect our lives on a profound level. The awakened person knows that these moments represent character-building chances to be grateful rather than regretful, courageous rather than timid, excellent rather than mediocre, compassionate and kind instead of judgmental and condemning.

In our limited awareness, sometimes we think that we've been given only one way to do something. Normally when interacting with someone else, we're taught to believe that whatever you do to me, I have to do it back to you. It's the eye-for-an-eye mentality. You hit me, I'm going to hit you back. You curse at me, I'm going to curse you back. But the higher intention, which is the other voice, says no. You can consciously choose to do things differently. You can start asserting that you want to know why you came here and began meditating on that all-important query. You can wake up in the morning declaring your intentions for the day. Once you do these things, you find that the answers to the questions you ask most diligently will start filtering softly into your awareness as well.

Picking Up the Pieces

After my football dreams came to such an abrupt, painful end, I wanted more than anything to figure out where I belonged. I wanted to know why I'd ended up doing what I was doing, rather than living out my dreams. Without any kind of clear vision for my life, I set out to do what most people do: make money at something I felt I could be good at and reasonably enjoy. So I went to work as a sales rep for IBM.

Right away, I started making a ton of money my first year out of college. In my second year, I made even more money. On the outside, everything looked great. But on the inside, I was empty. All I could think was, I should've been playing pro football. Two years passed like this until I got a call from another company asking me to come work for them in their new Atlanta office. I figured why not? I had nothing to lose. So I left IBM and moved to Atlanta.

I worked at the new company for a year, chasing down sales leads. We had a small office with three sales reps and a manager named Jim. Toward the end of the year, we got word that our sales territories were being changed and, for more than three weeks, we all discussed in detail which territory now belonged to which rep. That way there wouldn't be any confusion.

Feeling confident of our new arrangement, I set up an appointment at a company that I considered a particularly hot lead. I prepared diligently before actually meeting the client. Once I felt totally ready, I went over to the client's office and started my pitch. But after just a few seconds, the man held up his hand.

"Mr. Holt, hold on for a minute."

I said, "Yes, sir."

He handed me a document and said, "Isn't this your company?"

Confused, I looked down at the paper and then replied, "Yes, sir."

"We just got a proposal from a guy over there by the name of Jim."

Jim, the manager, was the same man who'd assigned us all our territories. That's when it hit me that he'd purposely gone behind my back trying to lure my client away. I was so embarrassed. Jim had made me look like an incompetent idiot. All I could say was, "Yes, sir, that looks like a proposal from us. I'm so sorry. I'm so sorry."

The client was gracious. "No problem," he said. "Yes, Jim was in here about two weeks ago."

"I'm sorry, sir. Thank you so much for your time," I said and hustled out the door.

I left that company with steam coming out of my ears. I stormed back to our office and burst through the door.

"Jim," I barked in front of everyone, "I need to talk to you! Right now!"

We went into his office and closed the door. That's when I went off.

"Look, don't you ever go into my *#!*% territory again without telling me! I just went to a potential client and you'd already given them a proposal. Are you out of your mind? Do you know it took us three weeks to get that appointment? You must know that because you were part of the process. So you must have gone behind my back on purpose. That's inexcusable!

"And you know what," I continued. "You're not even a good manager. You're not a 1990s manager—you're a 1970s manager! You wear high-waters. You're an embarrassment to me when we go into client's offices. You don't know how to talk the lingo because you start off trying to push people into a corner to make them buy something that they know nothing about and that's not the '90s way of doing business—it's a throwback to the 1970s and the way you did business back then. You're a 1970s manager, and don't you ever go into my client's office again!"

Jim stuttered for a minute, trying to get a word in, but I wouldn't let him. I was on a roll.

"This is about respect here, Jim. You have your job description. I have mine. Basically you are managing me, yes. I'm supposed to come back and give you reports on the territory. But by no means do you step across the line and do something out of integrity like that. It makes me look like I don't know what I'm doing in front of my customers, and I know what I'm doing. I've been trained—by the best! How dare you!"

During this entire exchange, my ego was right there, telling me that I was absolutely right. Let him have it! He deserves it! Looking back, I understand that my reaction came from the fact that I was angry because I didn't really want to be there in the first place. On top of that, the friend who'd gotten me the job was fired six months after I started. Jim was a rep with me when we opened the office. He was an older guy, so in my mind I decided, *They promoted the older guy, regardless of whether he can really do the job or not, and it sucks for me because Jim don't like me no way!*

So when Jim stepped out of bounds like he did, my first reaction was to think that he was trying to get at me. Rather than responding to the situation objectivity and compassionately, my intense reaction clearly came from my own mental garbage.

Not surprisingly, I got fired a month later.

In all fairness, I could've gone in and said, "Jim, what you did was very unprofessional, and I'm asking that you not do that again."

But given the situation, the first thing I should've done was taken a breath and become still. Of course, "I didn't. If I had, I probably would've said to myself, "I know Jim don't like me. But that's all right. It's not about that. There has to be a way for us to find common ground, at least enough to be able to work together." That way, the idea of him disliking me would not have been the headline of the intention for me to say what I said.

I also might have asked myself, "What's the intention behind my need to address him about this issue?"

From a clear space, it was obvious that the useful, necessary intention was to convey the fact that we must find a way to work productively together. I needed to convey to him that I was a man of excellence. When I went to see my clients, my interaction with them was of the highest integrity. It wasn't about Jim, and it wasn't about me. Not really. It was about the clients and making sure that they had access to the best that I, and our company, could offer.

Another thing I could've said to myself was, "I don't know if he likes me or not. I'm just not sure. But I don't really care." That takes the intention off the assumptions, which may or may not be true. Because for most people, their first instinct becomes, "Well, if he don't like me, I'm going to give him something not to like!"

Most of the time when you come out and tell somebody off or do something to make them feel bad, you're the one who ends up feeling empty inside. At least I do. This is what it looks, sounds, and feels like when you're controlled by the mental chatter. But when we step back and take a breath, we can practice going into the silence. In the silence, the voice can be heard clearly and unmistakably.

Stepping into the silence is one of the most difficult things I've ever learned to do in my life.

Chapter 5

Silencing the Angry Voices

Climbing Out of the Rut

I t took me many, many years—long after my interaction with Jim—to begin to recognize and more or less silence the mental chatter in my head that had controlled my thinking and my actions for so long. I simply got tired of feeling angry and frustrated for no good reason. If you're not living your life's purpose, waking up every morning full of enthusiasm and excitement about being part of something bigger than you are, it becomes all too easy to slip into these patterns of frustration, confusion, apathy, or anger. Some people just call it being in a rut.

"I don't know what I want to do with my life," you might be saying to yourself. "I work because I have to make money. I have to feed my family. But I'm not excited by what I do. I failed at living my dreams. I didn't become who I thought I was going to be. Now I don't know who I am or what I'm supposed to be doing here."

I've heard complaints like that over and over from people in all different walks and stations of life, even those most others would consider incredibly successful. There's no answer that I can give these people. Make no mistake—the answers are available. They're just not within me. The answers are waiting within the seed that lies at the core of our beings. The problem isn't that we don't have the answers to these dilemmas and questions readily available. We just usually don't know how to access them, because the truth that lies in the silence of our souls is obscured by the louder, angrier voice of ego chatter.

It took years of searching, learning, apologizing, and trial and error until finally I began to recognize my true self as something separate and apart from the noise in my head. At that point, I began to meditate on a regular basis. I found many exciting, inventive ways to meditate: sometimes through focusing on a beautiful painting by my friends Synthia St. James or Charles Bibbs. At other times, I would read a passage written by Maya Angelou or Sri Aurobindo, with my mind intent on the core meaning from which such beauty had come. At the end of the day, I would again heed the words of the divine to "take a deep breath and be with the silence and stillness."

When I first started my meditation practice, I'd wake up in the morning and say, "I do not want to sit here and just be silent! If I wanted to stay still, I'd go back to sleep. I want to get up. I need to use the bathroom. Okay, I'm going to do five minutes. That's all!"

And I'd just lay there. That's when I really began to notice the chatter. It took me the longest time to get to that place (I'm still getting to the place) where I can become still and the chatter is not constantly moving inside my mind. But when I first started meditating regularly, I was shocked. I thought, *Wow! There's a whole lot of stuff going on in my brain. Be quiet!*

I don't think a lot of people even know that they have mental chatter. I didn't. I identified with my thoughts, and it wasn't until I got still that I realized that everything from yesterday and the day before and years before would come to my mind in any moment of silence between thoughts. If I was watching television and saw something that sparked a memory, my mind would fly off on a tangent. Oh, God, I remember that when I was in New York. I'd think on it all night, go to sleep, and wake up in the morning, and that thought would still be in my awareness. Then, when I'd try to meditate, the thought would pop up in my head.

And a song would come with it.

Seriously. I'd be sitting there telling myself, "I love that song, but not right now… Well, okay, I'm going to let you play till the end." Then the song would get to the end, but it wouldn't end. And I'd think, *Hmm, that's interesting. You just want to take up my space!*

Once I realized that, I began speaking mantras like "God is all there is." And that made it harder for the chatter to get through. Once I started doing that, thoughts of what God is to me started coming to mind. I noticed the trees swaying. I saw people embrace one another. I watched life unfold from a different perspective.

In establishing a meditation practice, find what works for you. Perhaps you want to get a CD that has soothing sounds, which will put your mind in a state of calm and keep it constant on one thing as opposed to the chatter. Everyone's ego chatter will try to grab attention in different ways. For example, my ego loves to plan. It wants to make sure that my whole day is planned from start to finish. Okay, I need to get up, go to the bank, then go wash my clothes. I'll go to the post office while my clothes wash. If I have enough time, I'll get a quick workout in at the gym. Then from the clothes, what am I going to do? It goes on and on. During many points in my life, if I didn't have a lot of things to do on my agenda, there were feelings that came up that felt like depression.

In our society, if you're not doing something, you're called lethargic. Often, people use this constant busyness to convince themselves that their lives are important and meaningful. Busyness becomes a substitute for purpose. The feelings of aimlessness, depression, and inadequacy that can come up during fallow times are not signs that we need more busy work to keep us occupied. These are bright-red flags telling us that we need less busy work to clear a path in our minds and lives for the silence to speak to us about what we're really here to do.

When I lived in New York I also worked as a voice over artist in addition to being in *The Lion King*. I was highly sought after and had auditions every day up until show time. Even on my day off I sometimes had three or four auditions. There always seemed to be something waiting to be done. But when I moved to Los Angeles, I almost went crazy my first year because I didn't have all of that busy work to do. Anxious, turbulent thoughts continuously bubbled up in my mind. *You need an agent. You need a manager. That's what you need. You need to be auditioning for CSI!* Then of course I was worried about how to get the manager or agent to get the audition to book the job. I believed that it made me a worthwhile person when I was able to say, "I'm a working actor."

One day, Spirit said to me, "You have moved out here into

this vast silence that you're in now, and it's all good. Just take it in." Immediately my ego said, "No! I want to work! I don't want the silence. No! Blah, blah, blah, I can't hear nothing you say!"

I used all types of physical distractions to get away from the truth in the same way I used the mental distractions. If I didn't go to the gym over two days, my mind would start to play tricks. *Man, I don't know what's wrong with me! Oh God, I haven't been to the gym in so long. I'm so lazy! When was the last time I went to the gym? Well, let's see…what's today? Wednesday? I last went to the gym on Monday …*

One day, after subjecting myself to another one of these mean-spirited tirades, I heard a voice say, "You sound a little depressed." I responded, "I am! I need to be going to the gym."

"Why?"

"I need to keep in shape. Why do you think?" I quipped.

"Why?"

And that's when it hit me. I had a realization that literally stopped me in my tracks as I was on my way into a coffee shop. For the first time, I told myself the truth.

"Working out validates me. Having lots of things to do everyday validates me. I don't want people to think I'm lazy. I don't want me to think I'm lazy. And if I'm not doing something, I'm lazy."

"So you feel like a good, worthwhile human being only if you're busy working and being important and accomplishing something?"

"Yes, I guess so."

"What makes you think that? Do you think that you're not enough?"

"Yes."

That's where the dialogue with my ego began in earnest. Sometimes its good to pay attention to what's being said in your mental chatter. That way, you can challenge the hidden beliefs that may be operating in your life.

Eventually, I had to admit to myself that my deep-seated feelings of insecurity stemmed, in large part, from the fact that I allowed my athletic background and my physical prowess to validate me. I'd never learned to believe I was good enough without sports. The feeling was so intense that at the end of my college career, when I wasn't chosen to go pro and my dreams were shattered, I couldn't even watch football for the next three seasons.

I was used to being known as a champion, a star on the field and off. When that identity was so abruptly removed from my life, I'd been devastated, and part of me hadn't fully recovered. The shadow of unfulfilled dreams had followed me through jobs, career changes, and relationships.

"Sometimes I feel like I'm just not enough," I said to myself out loud.

I walked out of the coffee shop, jumped into my car, and bawled like a baby.

Once I'd fallen out of touch with the innate ability to validate myself from within, I'd spent most of my life forming another identity around outside influences. I'd allowed sports and working at IBM to validate me. I'd allowed other people's high opinion of me to validate me. My mother had always said, "Those other two children can tell me yes, but if that baby boy of mine comes and tells me no, I'm not going to do it. I don't care what it is." That identity is what I held on to. The identity that said, "People look at me. I am strong. I am the athlete. I am the smart kid, and I go to church every Sunday ..."

Meanwhile, Spirit was gently prodding me with the question: But who are you?

In the middle of my process, with tears streaming down my face, my ego started playing the blame game. (It's their fault I feel like this. They did this to me!) The ego was trying to distract my attention from the revelations that were coming through. Finally, the awakened aspect of me—that part of me that had always been enough and had never been hurt or harmed in any way—said to my ego, "Okay, you know I love you—that small little boy who thought his father didn't care about him. I love the adolescent who thought he needed to be more and he allowed sports to become his life. But clutching on to those identities no longer serves you. I know you're trying to protect me from being hurt. But is that really who you are?"

That's not who I was.

Contrary to what you may have heard or been taught, your ego isn't a bad thing. It means well. The ego wants to keep you safe, secure, protected, and accepted. The problem comes in because it usually attempts to do this by keeping you in the same small, reclusive orbit that you've always gravitated toward. Life, on the other hand, is about change, growth, and unfolding ever-greater aspects of the self. We all know the pain that is experienced when life decides to change even though you don't want it to. The harder you try to hold on to the comfort and safety of "what was" or "how it's always been done," the more pain you feel.

Eventually, I realized that I had to stop fighting with my ego. It was part of me, and I understood that truly loving myself meant loving all aspects of my self.

In meditation, I began to tell my ego, "I know you're only trying to protect me. I know that you're going to continue to try to protect me, but that no longer serves me. So I need to know if you'll join sides with this higher consciousness that's now looking to emerge through me."

Sometimes when the ego voice comes and says, "Don't go over there ... don't take a left, take a right," it's best to listen to it because that can be the voice of protection. Allow the ego to have its say. Also, if you reject the ego and continue to tell that voice to go away, then what you continue to resist will just keep coming back. That can be a tricky concept for some people who believe and have been told that the ego is bad and they don't want the ego around them. The ego isn't bad, but it is a force that can (and does) run things sometimes. You may have to tell your ego, "Look, you're going to have to work with me because the kind of protection you want to give me hinders my unfolding and growth. It no longer serves me. So you're going to have to lay off a little bit and be quiet and let me do my thing so that I can hear that other voice." At that point, the chatter that used to define you begins to quiet down.

Using the Chatter to Validate Who and What You Are

As it was in my experience, mental chatter quite often stems from people trying to validate themselves. It's the absence of *real* validation, which comes from knowing the truth about yourself. The truth is that you're perfect and whole just as you are and more than capable of following and fulfilling your deepest dreams. The ego, however, will use its power to try and talk you up on more superficial levels. It will try to use any situation that comes its way to make itself feel bigger. That need to validate can come from the most unexpected places.

If we aren't happy with who we are or where we are in our lives, we naturally seek validation from outside forces. No matter what's going on it becomes all about us. We wonder how we look to others, what they think, how we're being affected by a situation, how our best efforts are measuring up, etc. Sometimes we're conscious that we're behaving in this way, sometimes not. But when we're aware, we can honestly assess a situation and recognize if we're trying to validate ourselves rather than humbly assisting another who's in need.

As you're talking to your ego, you'll slowly begin to discern which thoughts and actions are coming from the chatter. You'll learn how to peel them away so that you can engage in spirit-driven right action, as opposed to ego-driven reaction.

In that process, there are some questions that you might want to ask yourself. One of the main questions is: Why do I do what I do?

Ask yourself why you do what you do. Why do you say what you say? Why do you talk a certain way around one person and then, when somebody else comes around, you talk like a totally different person. Why do you dress the way you dress? The ego will tell you things like, "You need to go get a new outfit. It's Easter, and everybody's going to have a new outfit." Then the conversation might go something like this:

"I know I'm not going to church without a new outfit on."

"Why?"

"Because I'm not."

"But why? Do you think people will know if you wear the same outfit you wore last year? Do you think it will make you a laughing stock because people will think you don't have any money for new clothes?"

"Well, now that you mention it…"

Or the conversation could go something like this:

"Man, I need a new car."

"The car you have runs fine."

"But I need a new one."

"Why?"

"Because all my friends have new cars, and if I don't have a new car, too, they'll all think I don't make enough money to afford a new car…"

When a person's actions are driven by vision and purpose, they radiate power. The fulfillment of the goals and dreams for which they were born becomes undeniable. These are very different than the goals and dreams that stem from the ego, which often need to be dashed in order to allow a greater vision the space to emerge. Case in point: My early football career. When a person's actions are ego driven, those actions tend to boil down to a need to hide the fact that they feel less than whole. In that circumstance, achieving, doing, and imitating are all different methods used to achieve external validation.

You talk a certain way to validate that you're cool. You dress a certain way to validate that you're attractive. It takes a leap of faith to move from using things to validate yourself to knowing that you are perfect and whole exactly as you are in this moment. Every culture has its benchmarks that people use to tell the world, "I'm special, I'm important." In one culture, it may be how many children you have. In another culture, it may be how many cars you have or what kind of house you live in or how many letters you have behind your name. Somewhere else it might be your family lineage.

No matter which things you use to validate yourself, they're still part of an external reality that, in and of itself, has no bearing on your worth or your truthful experience of the world. Once you make the choice to release that way of thinking, once you get into the mind-set of knowing that you have everything you need and the power to call it forth, you start becoming infinitely grateful for who you are. You cherish and respect what you already have. When you get more, you cherish that with love and gratitude, too.

From that space, it's much easier to see life objectively. Peace of mind and acceptance are by-products of that flow. With love, peace, and acceptance comes enthusiasm and vision. Dreams that seemed impossible—whether letting them go or finding the courage to go out and finally fulfill them—are now within your mind's grasp.

From False Ego to Full Realization

So, what is the real self that we're looking to access—the self that understands our deepest desires, dreams, and potentials; the

to this planet completely aware of its purpose
understanding of how to achieve it? Who is this
voice, that's been so effectively drowned out and
covered over by ego chatter and mental garbage?

Imagine waking up every day and saying, "Okay, I am divine
love on the planet. How does love look to me? I am divine peace
on the planet. What does peace look like to me?" Love, peace, joy,
harmony—they're all action words. They're not nouns as we've
been taught to believe. You may wake up and say, "Today I'm
going to shut my mouth when I know I shouldn't be talking. I'm
going to be a better listener today. In fact, I AM divine listening
and attention today." Then, when you walk out of your house,
you may find yourself in conversation with somebody who says,
"Do you know what happened to me?" At that point, he or
she starts running off at the mouth and you, too, find yourself
wanting to run off. But then you can stop and say, "I'm going to
listen fully to this person because I am divine attention today."

You never know what your simple actions are transmitting to
somebody else. Maybe because you stopped to listen, the person
that you were talking to said, "Somebody's really interested in what
I have to say. Wow." Or "that's what love feels like to me." You
never know how your living your life is affecting someone else.

This is about more than just being a better you, in the same
way that fulfilling your goals and dreams is about more than just
making yourself rich or happy. This is about being part of a
global shift.

Part of this shifting of awareness is stepping out on the faith
journey, where we continue to surf into the deeper waters and
venture into places where we've never tread in order to grow and

expand. The voice is the direct line that puts you in touch with the universal whole because it comes from the whole. It comes from the core. The voice allows us to increase our awareness, not only of ourselves, but of things and people everywhere.

Living life from that state helps you move into areas of inclusiveness, rather than exclusiveness. You get choices on how to become more sensitive to what's around you. You learn a deeper understanding of love, peace, generosity, and happiness. This path is not without challenges, of course. But even then, you know you have the ability to choose how you want to feel. If you're feeling sad, then know that the sadness has come for you to look at and deal with, that there's a time and a place to examine every emotion in the human experience.

If we look back in history, we've had avatars, great men and women who've stepped up and changed the world. Jesus was one of the greatest examples in human history. Buddha was another. Martin Luther King, Jr.; Mohandas Gandhi; Albert Einstein; Sojourner Truth; and Mother Teresa are all examples of modern sages. Through their individual consciousness, they led their people to the Promised Land, so to speak. Right now, we're all responsible for leading one another to the Promised Land. I don't believe that now is the time for us to wait for another leader to emerge whom we can look at and say, "Okay, here's all our baggage. Clean it up!"

We are the saviors.

What I mean by this is that we all have a responsibility here. It's time for each person to step up and say, "You know what? I'm pulling my load." If we're to continue in the unfolding that the divine wants for this planet right now, we'll heed the stirring that's happening everywhere to come forward and be heard, so that the emanation of God that's inside of you is revealed. This is what the voice is urging us to be and do. It's not saying reach out and look for another Buddha or reach out and look for another Jesus. It's telling us to look for that shift in consciousness within, to know that we're here by divine appointment. It's telling us to look at the works that the avatars have demonstrated on earth and know that, as the Bible says, greater works than these are we to do.

How do we become a healed society? Through me. How can my neighbor down the street be uplifted? Through me. How can a person living in another country experience love? Through me. If someone's going through the darkness, it's my turn to shine light for him or her.

How do the people in your life get to experience unconditional love, acceptance, and inspiration? Through you! Through the power and the brilliance that shines forth as you reveal ever-deeper facets of your true self.

When people say that we're in such a deficit and the world is crumbling and dying, we have to realize that all the people of the world would have to do is say, "I really am tired of war. And I'm tired of thinking, *I'm tired of war.* I'm going to do something about it because I want peace." The opportunity, then, is to access the consciousness to choose it. Will you have to wade through all your stuff to get to peace? Yes, probably. It's an inside job. When you choose to turn away from war, you must choose to take the next step and actively walk in the opposite direction.

When we say we want a beautiful, healthy, and clean environment for our children to grow in, it's our higher self that actually comes forth to take action to create that environment. This is the self that's willing to change, sacrifice, and learn a better way of being in the world that will benefit all of humanity. Are we willing to actively participate in supporting the environment by learning more about the effects we've had on the rivers, the mountains, and the trees? Our real self understands the symbiotic relationship we have with the rest of the planet and that protecting the planet is protecting ourselves. Causing destruction to the planet is destroying ourselves.

This journey toward accessing the awakened consciousness first starts with silence. We need silence. Our minds constantly are inundated with chatter, from within and without. It's everywhere in our society, from the time you wake up in the morning until you go to bed at night. As soon as you get online to type someone an e-mail, all these things pop up: Famous country star divorces cheating husband ...Who would be your presidential candidate? ... Thousands swear by new miracle diet! All of this stuff gets us off track. If you're not conscious, you'll find yourself at the computer a half an hour after you've turned it on, asking, "Hmm ... now what did I get online to do?"

The inundation continues to reinforce the negativity, craziness, and chaos that struggle to get your attention on a daily basis. I remember when I was living in the south, in Memphis, the headlines in the newspapers proclaimed, "Blacks and Jews Fighting in Memphis." Well, I'd never seen any of this so-called fighting. It wasn't true in my life or the lives of anyone I knew— whether they were black or Jewish. When we buy into these kinds of ideas, we allow propaganda machines run by exterior forces to dictate our experience. For example, people often believe whatever the media tells them to believe. "Man with Six Purple Eyeballs Spotted in Sedona, Arizona!" The next thing you know, you'll have people talking about, "Did you hear about the man in Sedona with six purple eyeballs?" Then, everybody's believing it.

This societal chaos gets added to your own personal chaos, which the ego is always happy to instigate. The things that matter to you—your dreams, your community, the healing of the planet, the growth and evolution of your soul—begin to recede as they're pushed back by the waves of meaningless noise.

We've been taught to believe in this noise because, embedded within it, are the cultural codes and cues that tell us whether or not we're in sync with the prevailing thoughts of our communities and our nation. These cues and codes tell us whether we're succeeding as good, worthwhile human beings in society's eyes. Unfortunately, most of these codes and beliefs aren't true! For example, our Western culture teaches: If you're not doing something, you're lazy. If you aren't capable of handling a thousand projects at one time, you are incompetent, insufficient, and not a good worker. You don't think. You'll never "make it" in life.

It can be scary stuff. No wonder people pull away from challenge and uncertainty, away from their goals and dreams. Feelings of isolation, separation, and inadequacy begin to seem normal. Many people are closed cans right now, looking over their shoulder, literally and metaphorically, holding on to whatever they think they own, whatever they think they are. They'll fight to the death if someone comes along who challenges their way of being in the world, even if that challenge would ultimately offer them something better. The fear behind this behavior stems from a false sense of reality and, more important, a false sense of the self.

When people are trapped in mental garbage, which causes them to think and act in these ways, they will lie to themselves and to others. They'll act in ways that aren't true to who they are, but that they believe will cause other people to say, "Oh, she's so nice." However, that's putting on a personality, not building character. Character is the truth of who we are. Building character is teaching excellence and perseverance. Unfortunately, so many people today seem to be willing to sidestep character to be nice, because if we're nice we can get by.

Anyone can be nice and mediocre. We're striving to be excellent. Part of the process of becoming excellent is embracing your real essence and accepting all aspects of your journey—set backs, failures, lost dreams, and all. The trick is, when you embrace your authenticity, when you begin listening to the voice of higher consciousness, all of the false notions and ego-driven dreams dissolve. What you're left with is a path into the heart of your own brilliance.

Chapter 6

Stepping Into the Unknown

When the Planted Seeds Begin to Grow

W hen chatter controls your mind, it's evident in every aspect of your day-to-day life. Confusion settles in. It becomes very easy to find yourself making decisions that aren't in the interest of your highest good. The manipulative voices that speak through the chatter originate not just from your ego, but from the egos of others who've told you things about yourself, or about life in general, that may or may not be true. More often than not, the so-called facts that others tell us aren't the reality, meaning they're not based in unchanging, universal principle. They're subjective impressions and perspectives. But as soon as we take these beliefs on as true, that's what they become in our lives. If we're to become free of the manipulations of the ego, there must be a consistent practice for grounding oneself in an objective reality, which operates beyond what our senses and emotions would lead us to believe. If not, the present moment of creativity and inspired action is easily lost. Negative thoughts are then free to grow, and they do so like weeds in our consciousness.

Someone may say to you, "You know, you're going to end up

in juvenile detention one day!" Then later on down the road, if you get into some trouble, those words may jump back up into your consciousness. Unbeknownst to you, you've set someone else's belief into motion in your life. Whether another person's negative thoughts have been thrust onto you or you've come up with them all by yourself, the results tend to be the same. Lost in the ego's perspective, you may find yourself saying things like, "I don't know what to do with my life .." "I don't think I have a purpose. I'm not that good at anything ..." "I don't know why I did that. It was so stupid!" "I feel so lost ..." "What do you think?" The seeds of fear and doubt have taken root, sprouting spiritual weeds all over the place.

Conversely, we also encounter people in our lives who plant seeds of wisdom inside our hearts. If we're compassionate and loving, we can do this for ourselves. The words we hear may not register in a profound way at the time that they're said. But eventually, if we're open, the truth that's been spoken settles in fertile ground in our consciousness and begins to grow.

The seeds that are planted within us, good or bad, are under our guidance. We get to water them. If I'm a young person, I can water the seed that says, "I'm going to be a juvenile delinquent," or I can water the seed that says, "I'm going to be a painter." It's all choice, whether we're making our choices consciously or not. The seeds that are most closely aligned with your beliefs and actions are the ones that are going to grow. We want to make sure that those seeds are also in alignment with our purpose and intention.

When people first take on the practice of setting conscious intentions, it's common for the word intention to become synonymous with the desire to achieve material goals. Ultimately, however, the most powerful intentions become ways of being in your life. For example, my intention as an artist is to create vehicles that will provide opportunities for other people to experience more of the joy and freedom that life has to offer. Being consistently mindful of that intention prompts me to check in regularly with myself to see if my thoughts and actions are in alignment with my purpose. My actions will then manifest as plays, concerts, CDs, books, films, speeches, and workshops. But the purpose, the intention to embody the spirit of love and generosity, comes first.

Our loving intentions bring us into harmony with our divine excellence. Some people would call it divine purpose, but I call it divine excellence because in every single thing we do, we get to operate at a very high vibration. If we're creating a book, we're not going to be content to just write some words on a page that we haven't lived. We won't plagiarize. Divine excellence says, "I want to give the world something that comes from the very core of who I am."

Setting powerful intentions can bring us into alignment with our potential to provide service to others, get clarity in our lives, and find right relationships. The most powerful intentions focus not only on you getting what you want, but also on sharing what you have. Individual desires are great. But when we all begin to share and manifest things together, it creates a much higher vibration that's capable of changing the world far beyond our individual reach, because we're contagious beings.

From this space, we can step into unknown territory. It's here that willingness and grace begin to magnetize experiences into our lives that are far beyond anything we could ever have dreamed up.

We're inviting a new paradigm into our awareness where we question our most basic desires: Why do you want what you want? Do you want power and security? Do you want to serve your community? Do you want wealth? Do you want to be in movies and television just to be famous? Or do you want the visibility to touch and change the world further. Your answers, no matter what they are, are capable of propelling you forward into uncharted territory.

Taking the Chance to Live Your Dreams

I can only speak of this journey because I've experienced it firsthand. When I left my home in Atlanta and moved to New York to be an actor with $400 in my pocket, I never could've envisioned the dramatic turn that my life was going to take.

Within days of arriving in New York, I was already hot on the trail to my first job. I woke up at 7:30 in the morning to make an audition for the Broadway musical *Rent*. When I got downtown at 9:30 a.m., there was already a line of people wrapped around the entire block. I took my place at the end of the line. For the next 10 hours, I inched my way to the hallowed theater doors, anxiously waiting for my turn to sing.

Many audition veterans had brought books, homework, and music to help pass the time. There was a group of about 10 ahead of me dressed in rocker outfits with their guitars, singing songs from the show as if they were in performance. While waiting in line, I had an opportunity to see why New York City was called the "melting pot" of the world. No two people looked or sounded the same. I'd heard at least ten different languages in the 30-minute subway ride to the audition. People seemed to be in overdrive and constant motion. Never in my life had I seen people in such a rush to get somewhere.

Eventually, the sun began to set, and I suddenly realized it was already 7:30 in the evening. I was within ten feet of the doors to audition. I thought, *Wow, I finally made it. I am getting ready to have my first audition in New York City!* I began my ritual of warming up my voice and taking deep breaths to keep from getting nervous. My legs were numb from standing all day, so I began running in place and shaking my arms and head—which seemed to be a better preparation for a track meet than a Broadway show. But I had to wake myself up.

The door opened, and I felt my body tense in anticipation. However, instead of inviting the next group of ten to come up-stairs to sing, the audition monitor announced, "At this time we're not seeing anyone else. Please leave your head shot and resume in the box, and we'll contact you if we're interested. Thank you for your time and patience."

No, this couldn't be happening. But it was. Immensely dejected, I walked through the Theater District on my way home. As disappointed as I was, the spectacle of Broadway and all its players was amazing. I began to picture the city as a perpetual fun house decorated with flashing lights, grand marquees, and fingers of fame all pointing at you through reflected mirrors. At the bottom of its doors are the words, "enter at your own risk" written in small characters.

I stopped at a newsstand and picked up a copy of the week's Backstage, which many consider to be the stage actors' bible in New York. I saw an audition call for singers for the national touring production of *Jesus Christ Superstar*. Instantly, I decided that I would be there.

There were a few things about auditions that intimidated me. The fact that I didn't have formal theatrical training, like the majority of my peers, played the largest role in my lack of confidence. To a newcomer, auditions in New York were like walking into a circus filled with contortionists. There were people stretching parts of the body in impossible directions that looked vaguely masochistic. The halls were filled with a different type of freak show going on at every corner. The restrooms were tuning chambers, every man and tune for himself. Never in my life had I heard such a symphony of chaos. Not without my bag of talents, I unabashedly jumped into the deep waters, once again. My saving grace rested in knowing that as soon as I sung my first note, the quivering in my body would somehow align with the melody of the song, and that the fear would soon dissolve.

The day of the audition for *Jesus Christ Superstar* had finally arrived, and I was beyond excited. I dedicated the entire morning to warming up my voice and body. Coach Fred Hill, my beloved junior high track coach would've been proud. However, about an hour before the audition, I noticed that my level of excitement had begun to fade. The closer the time came for me to leave to go to the audition, the more I thought about not going. It took me about 45 minutes to completely talk myself out of going at all.

I used every excuse for not going that I could think of: *It's not that important anyway … Auditions come a dime a dozen here … It's going to be another long line again.* I contemplated these thoughts for at least half an hour, and the chatter that was trying to dissuade me nearly won. Then I had a sudden vision that woke me up—me, on stage with Ted Neely, the original Jesus, and Carl Anderson who played the original Judas, singing to sold-out audiences and screaming fans from around the world.

"Are you out of your mind? How could you pass up this opportunity?" I asked myself.

That did it. I flew out the door and headed downtown, striding through the streets like a man on a mission. When I got there, I was thankful to see that the line to the audition for *Jesus Christ Superstar* was not wrapped around the entire block—only half way. I was one of the last in line, but the wait ended up being far less that half the day. In fact, the four hours waiting in line seemed to go by pretty quickly. As I entered the room to sing, I went straight to the accompanist to hand him the sheet music to the song I was going to sing, but at the last minute I asked his advice on singing something other than the song I had originally prepared. He suggested that I sing an anthem. I chose "America the Beautiful," and then proceeded with the audition.

When I finished, I knew that I must have done something right. The entire auditioning panel leapt to its feet and applauded.

Wow, I thought, *they must have really liked my performance.* That just shows how naïve I still was: I later found out that standing ovations were almost unheard of, and to rate one at a theatrical audition was quite extraordinary. After three rigorous days of callbacks by producers, directors, and choreographers, the production team narrowed the field down to 12 contenders— only 6 would be cast. I knew that one of them had to be me.

The Day of Reckoning

The show's producer conducted the final callback. At the end of the day, the dozen of us left waited nervously while the production team decided which six among us would be chosen to go on tour. I must admit that the wait seemed like an eternity. I could hear my mother's overly protective voice and my father's disapproving voice both fighting for space inside my head to see which one would get the privilege of telling me how crazy I was. I felt the heavy weight of that bickering and, for a split second, sank into a muddy dejection. But those words could only discourage my efforts for so long. I began to see them for what they were: powerless ghosts of the past. I realized at that moment that I had stepped beyond my comfort zone, out into a higher understanding and awareness.

I had to concentrate in order to breathe as the names of the chosen actors were read from his piece of paper: "Danielle, please stay. Eddie, please stay. Seth, please stay. Charles Holt, please stay."

I wanted to ask the person next to me, "Did he say 'Charles Holt, please stay'?" I couldn't believe it. In a state of hysteria, I immediately began calling family and friends to tell them the great news. I'd only been in New York for a month, and I'd already landed a national tour!

My character Simon had one of the hottest songs in the show. Each night of performance, I lost my self in the music, surrendering to the energy of the audience and the cast. I jumped around the stage hitting high notes, low notes, and everything in between. This experience brought back memories of me dancing for my parent's friends as child. The only difference was that everybody wanted to hear more, and nobody told me to go to my room. It made me realize that although my parents didn't understand the path I'd chosen and how performing made me feel, this time I couldn't keep quiet about it. I finally understood that this was what life and living were all about, and I knew that there was much more to come.

When You've Gotten What You Think You Want, It's Time to Go Deeper

After the *Jesus Christ Superstar* tour, I went back to New York. Within less than a month's time, I booked a role in the first national touring company of the show that had started it all for me: *Smokey Joe's Cafe*. It was amazing to see the vision that I'd held so long before come to fruition.

Then, once the run with *Smokey Joe's Cafe* came to an end, I found out that I'd booked a role in *The Lion King*. By this time, *The Lion King* had surpassed *Rent*, and everything else, as the hottest ticket on Broadway. People were calling it the most beautiful, innovative spectacle they'd ever seen. And I was going to be a part of that!

All my dreams were coming true ...

I had one month of rehearsal and, on December 17, 1999, I made my Broadway debut. There aren't words to explain what I felt as I walked down those aisles in our beloved elephant

Bertha's back leg. The costumes, the lights, and the energy: It's a feeling I wished every person could experience at least once, to get a taste of what being in a state of unparalleled ecstasy felt like. That one opening night alone changed my life.

I happily settled into my life as a Broadway stage actor and for years lived that role to its fullest. The pace of the city that had seemed so frenetic and foreign to me when I arrived soon became my normal pace. There was almost never an unscheduled moment in my day. Even my days off from performing on Broadway were filled with auditions and other acting jobs. My mind raced constantly, always trying to stay on top of what I needed to do next.

One day on the subway train, in a rare moment of stillness, I sat and listened to myself breathe. It was an epiphany for me. The thought came to me that in the years that I'd now lived in New York, I couldn't remember having ever taken a conscious breath.

This realization shook me deeply. As of yet, I hadn't had any experience with centering meditation, but still something inside me knew that a change was desperately needed. I had to admit that, even though I had everything I ever wanted and more, I was getting burned out. Somehow getting everything I wanted still wasn't enough. I'd achieved my greatest dreams. Where else could I possibly go from there?

The voice inside was quietly but consistently trying to give me answers and direction. I understood that my epiphany about the breath had something to do with it, but at that point I didn't understand what it meant. Clearly I'd been breathing all those years, whether I remembered it or not. But my mind was so inundated with appointments, what had happened the day before, what was going to happen the next day (or next week), where I was going for my vacation, how I did on my audition, what was going to happen after the show, what could possibly happen during the show ... As fast as those thoughts came to me, as fast as that chatter was in my mind, that is how I was breathing all those years. Quick, short, shallow.

As I was just beginning to learn, there's something about being aware in the moment, which changes that pattern. It opens you up to a much deeper level of connectedness and understanding. Consciously listening to your breath is a grounding experience. It allows you to settle into something, and that something is yourself.

As I said, this was quite an epiphany for me—and it was about to change my life completely. I just didn't know it yet. I was still too busy trying to figure out what it meant.

How Deep Can You Go?

Ultimately, the voice was showing me another variation of scripture that says, "It profits you nothing if you gain the whole world and lose your soul." It took me actually being able to live out my dream to discover that there was much more than what I had defined as a perfect life waiting for me. Once you've tasted success, especially if you've been struggling and striving for a very long time, it can be easy to fall into another kind of rut: The rut of complacency. Where you're at is way too comfortable for you to risk losing it by stepping out into unknown territory.

But the voice never admonishes us to stay in one spot and tread water, no matter how beautiful or comfortable that spot may be.

The voice was calling me to get still, breathe, and allow myself to plug into a much greater energy current than I'd ever experienced before. Allowing myself to breathe consciously into this life space helped me become aware, so that I wasn't being spun and run by the chatter in my mind.

I hadn't realized how deafening the chatter had become during my time in New York. The city was crowded with people rushing frantically to get wherever they were going. Whenever I got on the train, there were panhandlers. There were quartets singing. At every stop, someone was getting on saying, "Can you spare a dime?" Or someone was singing "One—one—oooone— hello! Daba daba doo doo dada doo doo dada do!"

Mentally, emotionally, and spiritually I'd become part of all of that confusion and chaos. As soon as I took the first conscious breath, however, I came to a space of peace where I still heard the noise but realized that I didn't have to listen and let it affect me. Conscious breathing gave me the ability to choose what I wanted to listen to, to go even deeper into my center—the place where true insight is gleaned and discoveries are made.

It's bliss when you first acknowledge and touch that sacred wellspring of peace. The silence fills the empty spaces within like water falling on dry ground. It allows you to step back from the turmoil, be it internal or external, so you can start filtering things. There's always going to be other voices. There's always going to be chatter. But you can get to the place where you can say, "Ah, I don't want to listen to that right now, and let it go."

Focused breathing allows you to reconnect with the inside, with the soul. It allows you to say, "You know what? I'm just going to take this moment and be with myself. I'll go in for just one minute, even though everything is happening around me, and I'll just breathe …"

Then other thoughts can come into that open space. You may find yourself thinking, *While I'm breathing, I'm noticing the people around me. And you know what? I bless them.* You realize that the breath that you're taking is the same breath that everybody else is breathing. It connects you with humanity. Instead of looking at the people as separate, doing their own thing, the centering breath helps make it clear that the other people all around you are just trying to make it, too. They're doing the best they can, just like you are. Everyone is alike in that sense.

This is a much more powerful state of consciousness from which to operate. It stems from knowing that we're all in this together. We're all in different stages of divine flow. Some of us just don't realize it. When we don't realize it, according to our experience, we ain't in it. We're in something else. But as soon as we switch, as soon as we change our minds, we can just jump right back into the healing waters that are the natural flow of universal energy within our being. It takes great discipline to stay aware of the fact that everything in life is unfolding divinely, even (and especially) when it doesn't seem like it.

If we were able to step back and view our individual lives from the larger perspective of the collective whole, we'd see that our lives are in perfect order. It's when we decide in our minds that things are wrong or bad that we feel disconnected from the Universal flow. As soon as I wake up in the morning, the universe is ready to have me experience something that I've never experienced before and allow me to look at life from a different, more profound perspective—if I'm willing. This is the choice that every one of us is given every day.

Some days I don't want to feel that connection. I don't want to go deeper. I don't want to step out into new, perhaps difficult or uncomfortable, territory. That's the victim energy, which says, "I'm not going anywhere. I'm staying right here where I know I've got it good. I've worked too hard to get here to even think about letting it go." But the other choice is to say, "There's something greater out there for me. I don't know what it looks like, but I can say yes to it and see where my yes takes me."

Your choice comes back to where you're breathing from. Is it the victim (complacent, in-a-rut) space? Or is it from a conscious state that asks, "Who am I really and what am I here to give?"

We must all ask ourselves which is more important: holding on to our victimhood or unfolding into that which we've come here to be? Ask yourself what, if anything, is keeping you from going deeper, from stepping out into your expanded self? What are you afraid you might have to give up? What have you worked too hard for to willingly let go of? What do you fear you will lose?

Most important, what do you stand to gain?

Chapter 7

Let's Be Honest

Holding On to Our Limitations

T he human yearning to lead a richer, more rewarding life is, on some level, universal. Our heart's desire is to live our greatest dreams and fulfill our highest potential. To ask questions like, "Would you prefer to be a victim or would you prefer to step into a great and powerful destiny?" seems foolish and simplistic.

But in reality, people fight to hold on to their limitations everyday. We stay in unfulfilling, sometimes poisonous relationships and convince ourselves that it's not really that bad. We never make good on the constant threat to quit that job we hate, because we've never even tried to find a better one. The doctor insists that we lose 50 pounds, and we swear that this time we're going to do it, no excuses—starting tomorrow. I've never met a person who hasn't engaged in this type of behavior in some way or another at some point in their lives. The question is, why?

Unfortunately, there's no easy, one-size-fits-all answer to the why question. There are as many different reasons as there are procrastinating, limited people. You may have been told things growing up as a child that have stayed with you your entire life, things like: "Never leave your family. You won't make it out there on your own." "The world is a hard, cold place. No one will ever give you anything." "I can do it by myself." "I can't do it by myself." "You think you're better than everybody else." "Money just doesn't come easily to our kind."

Many of these scripts are also thinly disguised cultural codes, such as: "I'm just a black man in a white man's world." "I'm a woman in a man's world." "I'm a big woman with a big nose, and no man will probably ever love me. I'll never be pretty enough."

When these themes come up and you're looking to release them, the trick is to mentally replace them with something else. But before you can do that, you must first silence the chatter. If a woman who believes that she's not attractive finds herself in the middle of a group and people start looking at her, the first thing she says to herself is, "Oh God, I wish these people would stop staring at me. I know how I look." That belief probably has nothing to do with the reality of the situation, but she creates it as reality by feeding into the chatter that tells her that it's the truth.

What is it that you've thought about yourself for years? What do you say over and over to yourself that's not necessarily true? When I moved to New York, I discovered that I had an issue with the way I talked. I told myself, "I'm from the South, and I talk like a Southerner. Ain't nobody up in New York gon' respect me because they think Southerners are ignorant." I'd heard that all my life. Did it stop me from going? No. But I still had to deal with the voice whispering in my ear that my twang made me inadequate in the eyes of all these new people I encountered. I vowed, "I ain't gon' open my mouth while I'm up there. I'm just gon' say yes and no. 'Cause I don't want these folks thinking I'm ignorant, 'cause I'm not ignorant."

I had to eventually ask myself what the thought of me being ignorant stemmed from. I concluded that it wasn't about someone else thinking I was ignorant. I'd created that thought in my mind because I believed that I was, on some level, socially inept compared to others. I couldn't blame it on "them." I had to face some hard truths and ask myself what made me think that I was ignorant? When did I start developing the belief that "I must be a dummy?"

Look honestly at what the major themes are in your life. Have you developed a false consciousness that allowed you to believe in unhealthy assumptions? Now close your eyes and breathe. All the chatter that comes up will tell you when it started. Ask yourself if you really believe whatever your personal script is? If you don't believe the negative themes that have shown up in your life, ask yourself how to release them once and for all. If you do believe the negative themes, ask yourself why. Do you want to believe limiting things about yourself and your capabilities? The answer in most cases will be, "No, I don't want to believe that about me."

Create your world, then.

When you recognize and heed the voice of truth, you're starting to get closer to who you really are. Maybe you haven't heard the voice of truth in years. Maybe you've chosen to build your life around what other people have said about you, both the good and the bad. But the voice of wisdom inside you says that you're greater than you've ever imagined yourself to be, and your conscious participation can change the world. It's going to take some work, but just continue to breathe. Breathing is the foundation that allows us to take a moment to be present with ourselves. It allows us to then acknowledge the chatter and ask, "Is that really what I want to hear?" If it is, then continue to allow the chatter to run your life.

But if its not, then try asking this question: If there were no limits on your life, if anything and everything was possible, what would your life look like? What would be different and what would be the same? What do you want to have? What do you want to be? These last two are inexorably intertwined because you can't have anything that you aren't first willing to become. Life doesn't work like that. Asking for something that you're unwilling to embody is another form of separation.

Once you tap into the thought of doing things differently, you realize that to consistently make higher choices is a process of building spiritual muscle. For example, suppose you receive the thought, *I'd like to have peace in my life. I can see myself living in peace and harmony with everyone around me.* The next thought that might come forward is, *How can I be peace? How can I be full of peace in my home and my job? How can I be peace on the street? It's my choice not to let other people upset me when they do things that I don't necessarily like.*

If you're like the average person, the muscle of unconscious reaction has been overworked for most of your life. That muscle has been validated and, in most individuals, continues to be fed on a regular basis. But now you've become aware of this new muscle of conscious creation. The question then becomes how to feed and strengthen your creative muscle as well.

Please keep in mind, this is not about being perfect or living a perfect life. It's about allowing life to live perfectly through you.

Allowing life to live through you is a whole lot easier and more joyful that trying to force life to conform to your will. When you try to do it the forceful way, the process begins to feel overwhelming. It often seems simpler to give in to the chatter than fight to reach some impossibly lofty vision of success. The frustrating part is that other people appear to have attained it: Beautiful homes and cars, a gorgeous spouse, lots of money, a great job. (Hint: Someone out there is also looking at something that you have or do and thinking the exact same thing about you—that you have "it" and they don't). If other people can do it but I can't, the logic goes, then there must be something wrong with me.

There's a widespread belief in the lie that, "There's a perfect life out there somewhere, and if I'm bigger, better, stronger, richer, smarter, or prettier, then it will come to me." Often this belief comes from the fact that people describe what's perfect by someone else's standards. My neighbor has the better job and is able to earn more income, so that he and his family can live in the bigger house. And now they're moving into an even bigger house in a better neighborhood. When my neighbor gets up in the morning to go to work, he drives the better car. People respect my neighbor more than they do me because he has it all together and I'm still struggling with so many different things... So we're busy comparing our lives to someone else's. It comes back to the success factor: What is success to me? If I'm not successful, then I'm not perfect enough. Something is missing form this paradigm.

A lot of the institutions within our society support that version of ourselves as less than. When I was in the Pentecostal

Church, I never felt good enough. I always had some type of demon that needed to be cast out of me. And if you have a demon, surely you can't be perfect before God.

Our church had a demon for every ailment: Overly tired? You got a sleep demon. Can't get to church on time? You got a tardy demon. You think what I'm saying is funny? You got a laughing demon. If the girls wore bright clothes or colorful earrings, they had a Jezebel demon. If you even thought about playing cards, you had that card-playing demon. You were never good enough.

When I was playing sports, I often felt (or, should I say, chose to feel) that if I didn't get a first down or a touchdown every time I touched the football, I didn't do well. I'd beat myself up. I should've run harder! I should've run inside instead of outside. He shouldn't have tackled me! That's what was driving me, the voice in my head that constantly said, "That wasn't good enough." If we outscored the other team 13 to 10, I'd still be unhappy because we should have beaten them 40 to 10. My performance wasn't good enough! I didn't give my all.

But the truth was, I had given my all in that moment.

I may have needed to practice some more, but that didn't mean that I wasn't good enough. In the larger picture, I did a perfect job in that moment, flaws, mistakes, and all. If I gave it everything that I had—or if I didn't give it all that I had—it was still perfect. Because the situation then had the opportunity to become a tuning fork. I could've asked myself: "Is this the way I want to live my life? Is what I just did representative of who I really am? Is there more within me?"

Anybody can be mediocre. If that's what I choose to do, then that's all right. But if I want to live the excellent life, I'll be encouraged to grow. This growth doesn't happen from a place of fear and doubt, but from a place of enthusiasm and willingness to give my all. At some point, I'll be asked to step out into the unknown, in order to live the truly excellent life.

The excellent life supports you and the world community. It's the light that shines in all of us, though it is brighter in some than in others. Many allow their light to dim by settling for mediocrity. The light of excellence is inspiring and ever-evolving. It doesn't engage in ridicule or judge us for not being good enough. The light of excellence lovingly and truthfully invites us to grow from wherever we are into a space of brilliance. It asks us to become on intimate terms with our own personal best.

We all came here to shine that greatness. We don't access it by trying to live a perfect life, meaning setting our standards by someone else's. The chattering voice will try to torment you into being perfect by flogging you with the fear of not being good enough. The voice of truth, on the other hand, calls out to you in a supportive, non-judgmental way. Yes, I could have gotten a first down on that play, and I didn't. It's okay, because now I know how to execute that play better, and I know I'll make a first down next time.

When the voice of guidance is speaking to you, it envelops you in a space of gentleness and unconditional love, inviting you to take a breath and reassess your position. The chattering voices swallow you up in the agitated, breathless feeling of insecurity that comes with being condemned. There's something about feeling blamed and condemned that is intimately linked to shame. You'll know the difference between the competing voices because they'll either shame and blame you, or give you the opportunity to take full responsibility for whatever has happened.

There are many ways to allow life to live perfectly through us, even though life may not look perfect by the definition and standards of others. The first thing is to surrender to life and make the choice to not get attached to the way we think life should look. To surrender to that extent takes some more building of your spiritual muscle. It means not blaming others, but taking full responsibility for the things we do.

Surrender is the by-product of breathing and meditation and being willing to ask: "What is trying to emerge through me? How can I be a benefit to this planet? How can I be a benefit to myself first, because I've made some bad choices in my life? I'm ready to change that now. So how can I be a better person to me?"

The Healing Power of ... You

It can be tough to continue to go deeper and deeper with this line of questioning. This type of spiritual cleansing requires faith and strength of purpose. The healing that arises from this kind of willingness will transform every aspect of your life.

But what if we don't want our entire lives transformed? We don't necessarily struggle against—or want to lose—all of our limitations. Just the ones we don't like right now. Some limitations can feel quite comfortable. We don't necessarily want a whole lot of spiritual growth if it looks like it might cost us our money, our standing in the community, or our important job. When you think you have the perfect life that we talked about earlier, you may not necessarily want to rock the boat.

But an integral part of this journey is opening up to something greater than our individual desires and perceptions by agreeing to participate in the cultivation of good outside of your self. If we gloss over that necessary step in the process of our spiritual and creative unfolding, it can cause us to be very selfish. So often you hear people proudly saying some variation of, "I can make a whole lot of money with my gift, and as long as I'm making a whole lot of money, life is great." But what if the people who really need your gift don't have a lot of money at all? What if the people who desperately need to experience your healing power (because all gifts have the power to heal) live in a developing country or in a ghetto or a prison? Would you be willing to participate and give your light as a true gift, without ever attaining some kind of monetary value?

Using the talents that one has at one's disposal to make money and function in society is, of course, a necessary aspect of life. But we're talking about being part of the unfolding of spiritual transcendence that is happening on the planet. We're talking about being a part of the transformation of someone else's life. Once you access your own greatness, its time to step out of your boundaries and share with others.

However, many people believe that they're going to lose something by doing that. Or they think that they're hindering themselves from gaining more money. But what about those people who need to experience your gifts and talents because it may be part of the process that's going to help them heal?

This can be a touchy subject. The worry is that if you just

follow your heart and give your gift away, what's left for you? We must reprogram that mind-set! The greater spiritual truth is that whatever you give away, you get to keep. The universe is limitless, and when we're tapped into a limitless source, every single thing that we give away makes room for more of what we just released to come through us.

Now, it goes without saying that people in the world experience scarcity every day. Some don't have money to buy food to eat. Some don't have proper clothing or housing. Others live in areas where their water sources are muddied and polluted with toxic waste. Here in Los Angeles where I live, amid all of the ostentatious wealth and beauty, is a city of homeless men, women, and children numbering more than 80,000—over twice the number of homeless in any other city in the United States. Poverty, lack, scarcity, and the fear of not being able to hold it all together seem to be everywhere you look.

How, then, can anyone credibly say that there's always more than enough for everyone?

To make that suggestion, we must define what it means to experience lack or scarcity and then redefine what constitutes wealth. If I ask someone who's homeless or broke to share their gifts, share their wealth, probably the first thing they're going to say to me is, "I don't have any money."

But since when does wealth automatically equal money?

In Western society, we're trained to see money and power as the only kind of wealth that matters. People love the idea of living in a society where, if they work really hard, they have the potential to make lots of money and buy a huge house and maybe a $200,000 car. But people who are striving toward that goal generally don't stop to consider that maybe one person in ten million is driving a $200,000 car. There are many, many more people working for minimum wage or close to it. Most of us work for the guy in the expensive car, and it's our collective labor that allows him to continue to make his payments. Yet we keep striving for more, running on the treadmill. However, the motivating idea that, "One day, if I keep working and striving I'll attain all that I desire," carries with it the subtext that, "I will be better if I have these things. Then people will envy me. They'll see who I really am and admire me and want to be like me."

Believing that money and power equal true wealth breeds fear in both the rich and the poor. It activates the desire to hoard what is felt to be most precious. People keep working and striving for the wealth that they think will bring them joy (which is really what everyone actually wants) and that somehow giving something away brings them further out of alignment with their goals.

To put it simply and honestly, the bottom line for most of us is, "I have to make a living. If I give away what I have, or if I follow the voice into some crazy, far-off place, which has no practical application, then I'm going to be destitute and unable to sustain myself, and nobody will want to be around me."

We must change our paradigm for what it means to be truly wealthy and successful.

Now don't get me wrong, having money is a wonderful thing. It's as wise and necessary to be in the flow of reciprocity when it comes to abundance as it is with any other spiritual quality. The universe itself is a manifestation of limitless abundance, and we are part of that. Prosperity is part of the nature of our being.

Being one with this divine good will not only heal me, but all those who come into contact with me. This is what living the good life is really all about. Once I consciously access the healing power of goodness and creativity within, it's my responsibility to share it and release it, making room for the next wave of goodness to come.

The Answers to All Life's Questions Are Right Here

Money. Success. Power. Love. Living a rich and fruitful life. These are the things that we seek to experience. When they don't show up in the ways that we think they should, it can cause great pain and consternation. But how do we invite these things into our lives in a more meaningful and abundant way? And if it were that simple, wouldn't we all have done it by now?

I guarantee that you already know the answers to these questions. In fact, you already know the answer to any question that you can possibly ask yourself. You already know how you can have life and have it more abundantly, as the scriptures say—right now.

Your answer lies in the asking. When we ask, the answers always come back to us, without fail. Unfortunately, we tend not to ask the right questions. Sometimes we're afraid to ask anything meaningful at all. The most common response to a dilemma is to go on autopilot and just do what we think will alleviate the discomfort and get ourselves back to our normal state of equilibrium by the fastest route. Or we just assume that we don't know what to do, thus allowing confusion, inertia, and/or panic to settle in. This is particularly apparent when it comes to deep issues such as such as money, love, success or spiritual awakening.

When we have the courage to face our truths fearlessly, our light shines ever brighter. In surrendering to the power of our light, somewhere along the journey (because we are lights to one another) our paths will cross somebody who's been struggling. Then our testimony can help in their shift in consciousness. We have all been privy to grace through someone else's perseverance and triumph. It's another level of revelation.

Through the power of surrender, it becomes possible to access the lasting riches of life; we love, share, and shine our light generously. We live abundantly in healthy relationships and as part of thriving communities. We can be honest with ourselves about our attachments to our perceived limitations, being willing to let them go and stay open to a larger idea of what constitutes a worthwhile life. That's a huge part of the process: surrendering our ego's vision of what success, or even spiritual growth, looks like. Once you release the way you think things ought to be, you can embrace the humility and willingness that accepts things the way they actually are. It's allowing yourself to stay open to the divine perfection of what's trying to emerge rather than trying to squeeze life into a tiny box of your choosing.

Chapter 8

Having the Courage to Surrender, to Shine, and to Share

Surrender

The concept of surrender is so vitally important to any spiritual journey that it warrants being examined in greater depth, especially since the concept is so widely misunderstood. Usually, the connotation behind the word *surrender* is to lose something or give up something of value without receiving anything in return. But nothing could be further from the truth. From a spiritual vantage point, surrender has everything to do with releasing something of a lower nature, whether it be a person, a thing, a concept, a belief, or a way of being, to make room for something greater to take its place.

Let me share an example that happened in my own life.

It's Time for a Change

In October 2003, while still in the cast of *The Lion King,* I spent my entire two-week vacation in Los Angeles. I knew that the visit to the City of Angels would be fun, but I didn't know that such a profound life lesson awaited me there.

A friend of mine in New York had arranged for me to meet some of her friends in the music business. I'd been trying desperately for three years to find somebody to commit to producing an album with me. All roads had thus far dead-ended, and I was willing to travel halfway across the globe to meet someone vaguely interested. My friend had made several meetings before I arrived. Each meeting seemed promising and gave me the opportunity to make new connections. At the end of the vacation, I was on such an emotional high that I had thought of a hundred ways to try and resurrect my music and get it started on a new, fresh track when I returned back to New York.

On the day that I was leaving to travel back East, I recall the plane taxiing to the runway for the takeoff. Seating was odd for me because I always requested aisle seats, but I ended up in a seat by the window. Absently, I listened to the usual safety announcement by the attendant with my mind a million miles away.

As I stared out the window, I heard the voice speak to me: "It's time, Charles. It is time."

Perhaps if I hadn't heard those words years before my *Lion King* campaign (eight shows a week I heard Rafiki tell Simba, "It is time!"), I would've thought that I was crazy. Like that moment in Atlanta long ago, I knew the voice and I knew what those words meant. Without giving it lots more thought, as soon as I returned home I began looking for a vehicle. Two months later, I purchased a hefty SUV, and five months after that, I submitted my letter of resignation to *The Lion King* management.

As with my move to New York, I had no idea what was about to unfold in my passage to Los Angeles. But I surrendered fully to the spirit of guidance, which told me that something beautiful was waiting for me there. It let me know unmistakably that it was time for me to dive into those uncharted waters once again.

So I sold all my furniture, said my good-byes, and packed the rest of my belongings. I dreamt of landing a role as a series regular on a prime-time drama and a starring role in the next blockbuster movie. I flew from New York to Nashville, where I'd shipped my belongings, picked up my new car, and began driving cross-country, through Memphis, Dallas, Albuquerque, and Salt Lake City, stopping to visit family and friends along the way. It ended up taking me seven days to complete the trip.

The last leg of the trip was 11 hours from Salt Lake City, and it seemed to be an eternity. Exhausted from the drive, I arrived in Los Angeles on September 12, 2004, at 10:30 p.m., looking forward to spending the rest of the night in my new apartment. But before I arrived there, my roommate, who'd appeared in *The Lion King* with me in New York and moved to L.A. six months before, called to tell me that we wouldn't be able to move in until the following day because the newly refinished floors weren't dry. He offered me the couch at his friend's house, but I opted to spend the night at a really swank Beverly Hills hotel for the evening. I figured I'd reward myself by getting a good night's rest at a really nice hotel.

The next morning was the start of a whole new chapter in my life.

The beautiful California sunshine beamed through the window in my cozy hotel room. I jumped out of bed, got dressed, and rushed down stairs to get in my SUV to drive to my new home. When I got downstairs, however, my car wasn't where I thought I'd parked it the night before. I looked and looked, thinking I may have parked it in another space a little farther down. It had been an exhausting trip, and I could've easily misjudged my parking space. I search everywhere, and still no car.

As a last resort, I asked the lady working at the front desk if my car could've been towed. She assured me that the likelihood of my car being taken from the grounds without someone at the hotel knowing was highly unlikely. Then it hit me like a ton of bricks: My car—with everything that I owned inside—had been stolen.

Thank you, L.A., I thought. *What a way to welcome me to your city.*

As the women at the front desk called the Beverly Hills Sheriff's Department to come issue a stolen-car report, I took a few deep breaths, concentrating on the theme I'd taken on for the year: character. I took another deep breath, closed my eyes, and raised my head and my hands to the sky. I made a declaration to myself and to the universe right there in the parking lot:

"I am here in Los Angeles, not by chance. I am here because I know in my heart that I am supposed to be here: Right here and Right now! There's no thing or circumstance that can keep me from what I came here to get!" As I released these words, I felt the force of energy surge through my body. I literally felt like I was at the center of the Universe, and that all around me was an ocean of goodness.

In spite of what happened, I found the courage to be thankful for making the trip all the way across the country to Los Angeles, safe and intact. I vowed then I wouldn't leave because of one disappointing setback. I chose to take the high road—the higher consciousness—and promised myself that when the sheriff arrived to issue the stolen-car report, I'd act as if I knew that everything was all right.

In the act of surrendering to the situation exactly as it presented itself, a new dynamic was set in motion. An opening was created, which allowed grace to take over. The voice of divine grace and peace came to me in that hotel parking lot and showed me clearly that I was much more than my possessions. In fact, by having everything that I owned stripped from me, I saw that there could be great liberty and joy in making a completely fresh start, with none of the remnants or baggage from the past to keep me anchored in the life that was. Would I have liked to have my things back? Of course I would have. However, the lesson for me in that moment was that I didn't need any of it back. I was just fine, exactly as I was.

The greatest truths and lessons quite often lay within the greatest challenges that we face in life. However, to extricate the wisdom of insight from the pain of experience, we must be willing to stop, be still, and listen for the guidance that comes from the voice of higher consciousness. We must be willing to listen and then surrender to the greater good that is always inherent in what we hear.

Another Road to Surrender

When we surrender, we're called into action from a greater level of awareness. We're urged to move forward boldly, to share the gifts and talents that we've been put on this planet to give. This last part is key, because, as we have all heard, faith without works is dead. We can hear, but if we don't surrender and actively participate in the unfolding of our good, it'll never happen.

Four years after I first moved to Los Angeles, I found myself at another crossroads in my life. I was being called to surrender to a new way of being that would allow me to give my talents and gifts to the world on a much larger scale. I, however, had other plans.

When a lesson is important enough, it always comes back to you, to make sure that you've understood what you needed to learn. Being someone who always needed to feel in charge, surrendering was somewhat of a challenging concept for me to grasp. I tried so hard for so long to do it my way, meaning my ego's way, only to find myself mired in pain and confusion.

In the spring of 2007, I heard Dr. Michael Bernard Beckwith speak at a Sunday service about living a life of ease and grace. That sounded great to me. I thought, *You know what? I'm working hard, waking up every day making 40 or 50 calls, trying to book my one-man show in all these different places. Maybe getting a couple of return calls. I definitely want to give up this struggle and accept divine ease and grace into my life. I want people to call me up and ask me to be in shows for a change.*

I'd always had issues with allowing myself to accept help from others. I was ready to contribute to somebody else at a moment's notice, but it was very hard for me to let people reciprocate. When others tried to contribute to me, I'd misconstrue it and the chattering voice would say, "No, you're trying to take me over! You're trying to take something from me, and I'm not going to let you do that. I have to protect what I've built for myself."

I recognized that limitation and finally said, "I'm surrendering to my life looking another way. I'll allow people to contribute to me, and I know that no one can take anything from me."

Something told me that things could be different if I'd let them be. The voice said, "Somebody is being sent to assist you in the process of getting your artistic message out to the masses. Can you give up the idea that you always have to do it all by yourself?"

And I replied quite emphatically, "Yes, I can!"

In theory, it sounded great. I prayed to let divine ease and grace enter my life. But then, instead of opening up to receive the answered prayer, I went right on about doing things the same old way I'd always done them. I held on to the need to do it all by myself.

Usually, I'd have dozens of universities and theaters lined up for the months ahead. But this particular summer I was struggling to confirm just a few. I hit a very painful brick wall. Nobody was returning my phone calls, and I was beyond frustrated with the whole process. Month by month, things just seemed to keep getting worse.

I spent nine months in a spiritually intense, emotionally dark space in my life. Unlike other times, when I had felt the sting of depression, this feeling lingered like a perpetual, thick haze of smoke. I created painfully dull moods in which I lived for days.

On an unusually sticky July afternoon, I sat on the couch, deciding whether or not to take a nap. That option seemed much more inviting than sitting in a hot living room in meditative silence. Even though I was still in resistance, I opted for the meditation, positioned my body in a yoga posture, and closed my eyes. As I began to breathe through my drowsiness, the voice began to send paragraphs of messages to me.

"Don't you realize that what you asked for has arrived? It's all here. What a glorious time for it to arrive!"

"What's arrived?" I asked.

"You asked to travel the world and share your gifts and talents. You said you wanted to be a pioneer in the unfolding goodness that is happening on the planet. You said you desire to be an agent for global transformation and live in a world that works for everyone, didn't you?"

"That's right. I asked for all those things."

"Well, your wish has been granted. You've now stepped farther into your greater yet to be, Charles."

"Oh my, God!" I groaned.

All that I'd asked to be a part of was at my doorstep. Knock. Knock. Knock. It didn't look like I thought it would. But then again, the agent of transformation comes in whatever form it wishes. It was time to put up or shut up. I realized then, there was no returning to my old way of existing. I had no choice but to surrender. I'd stepped over a rather deep threshold into a consciousness of expanding goodness. Even if I'd tried to turn back, I couldn't. I now knew what the ancestors meant when they said, "I come this far by faith, and there ain't no turning back." The tide of revelation is irreversible. This was the most challenging shift I'd ever encountered in my life—but I was ready. I looked at what had already taken place in my journey. All roads had led me to this place. It was time for me to once again put into practice what I knew to be the truth of who and what I am.

All I could say was, "Oh, wow. I've stepped into what I asked for and didn't even know it." That's the reason I'd felt like I was hitting a brick wall all of those months. I really couldn't move any farther. It was my time to say, "I surrender." I was hardheaded about it because I kept trying to push through *This is going to work, because this is the only way that it's worked in the past,* I'd thought. But even when I made a little progress, right away my path would get shut down completely. When Spirit tried to lead me down a better path into the unknown, I'd refused to go.

In effect, the brick wall was my answered prayer, preventing me from doing the things that I already knew wouldn't work and didn't make me happy but that I crazily insisted upon repeating. Spirit said, "You asked for this, and now what you asked for is trying to emerge through you. Let it. Let it come right now. Just give in."

It took such a long time before I followed the gentle urging in my soul, because the chattering voice was there saying, "But that's the way you've always done it. It should work. Why isn't it working this time? You're not trying hard enough! You must not be getting up early enough. Everybody that you're trying to contact on the East Coast is three hours ahead of you. The people in the Midwest are two hours ahead. No wonder you're not getting anywhere. You should be on those phones by 6 a.m. at the latest. Other people do it, and they're successful. What's wrong with you?"

Absolutely everything came up to try to keep me from hearing the truth: I was living my answered prayer.

For months, I stubbornly held on to "my way" of doing things. When I finally gave it up, I said, "God I can't do it like this anymore. I don't want to do it like this anymore."

During the month of November, I'd gotten on a plane in Chicago, and the plane was held at the gate waiting for a group of passengers whose connecting flight was late. The last passenger to board was a rather tall, weary-looking woman. She rushed onto the plane and slumped into the seat located in the row directly in front of me, near the window. During the entire flight, she kept looking back at me. We got off the plane, and I headed toward baggage claim, only to look over my shoulder and see this woman walking right beside me.

She finally turned to me and said, "Look, I know you're going to think I'm crazy, but I'm not. When I was on the plane, God told me I needed to know who you are. And I already know one thing about you."

I cautiously asked, "What is that?"

She said, "You're an entertainer."

I admit, I initially thought she was a bit strange, but that didn't deter me from engaging her. I gently smiled and said, "I am," and gave her a copy of my CD and told her about my one-man show based on the life of the author Richard Wright. She called me the next day and said, "I need to meet with you. Meet me for coffee."

We met up shortly after our conversation that same day, and she said, "When I first saw you, I knew that we were supposed to work together. I don't know how. But I'm a professor at Western Kentucky University, and I've just been thrown into promoting artists outside the country. I just got back from Cypress, Greece, and Turkey with a group of singers. I missed the plane that I was supposed to be on, and that's how I got on the plane with you. So I know it was a divine encounter, just like I know that we're going to work together. I don't know how, I just know we will."

We said our good-byes, and I didn't hear from her again for another three months. Then, in February, I got a call on my way to the Super Bowl in Phoenix (New York Giants vs. New England Patriots). I was blasting the music in my car so I hadn't heard the phone ring. When I finally saw the red alert light flashing, I listened to the message. It was the "nutty" professor from Western Kentucky. I immediately called her back.

She said, "Look, my headline storyteller has backed out of the next gig in Turkey. We have two or three weeks before we have to go. I have to come up with somebody to replace her. I prayed about it last night, and the first name that came to me was Charles Holt. Can you do it?"

I immediately said yes. I had no script whatsoever. I wrote the script in my head while riding in my car to Arizona. I decided that I'd do a show about the community where I grew up. Lake Providence was a small community located in the southeastern quadrant of Davidson County, Nashville, Tennessee. A gentleman by the name of Larry A. Thompson founded the town in 1868. Reverend Thompson was a missionary, and he stumbled upon this land, all weeds and bushes. Rev. Thompson looked over that seemingly barren land and declared that day, "Right here, I'm going to build my church, and I'm going to call it Lake Providence Missionary Baptist Church, 'cause it is the providence, the divine direction of God that has brought me here." People began settling there, and eventually an entire community sprung up around that place. On the town's northern border was a flowing creek where new converts were baptized— my grandparents included. I am technically fourth generation, but because I am so many years younger than my brother and sister, I classify myself as a fifth-generation product of that vision, which encompasses a town that's now a historical landmark.

Two weeks later, I was on my way to Turkey.

The trip was yet another personal moment of enlightenment. More important than the trip being a success was the impact of being in a country and amongst people I knew very little about. I left Ankara with a burgeoning attitude of gratitude and humbleness. I had the opportunity to perform for nearly a thousand students at Ankara's oldest high school, as well as one of Turkey's most prestigious universities. The most memorable part of the entire trip was when a woman who was interviewing me for a Turkish television show prior to a performance said, "Charles, you give us courage." I paused, smiling at her and the splendor of what she had just shared. An overwhelming feeling of humility showered over me as a brilliant glow seemed to shadow her beautiful face. I knew right then and there that everything that I'd experienced had served as a beautiful orchestration to get me to the place where I could be a blessing to someone else.

When we surrender to the unknown, what emerges through us are the gems that have been hidden for so many years. They're uncovered because we don't have the mental chatter concealing them. We begin to step into that which we surrender to. This process is the exact opposite of the fatalistic type of mind-set that says, "I give in because nothing is going to change anyway." The main difference between fatalism and surrender is that true surrender ushers in a greater emergence.

In order to fully surrender, it requires releasing judgment on what things should look like. I didn't think that grace and ease had come into my life, because they came in a form totally different than what my mind told me they should look like. Then I kept bumping head up against my idea until the voice of spirit within me finally said, "Look, dodo, you asked for this. This experience has come to help you through your next stage of emergence. Can you see it now?"

That's the gift in the whole process: The present and the present. You become acquainted with the humble, moment-by-moment state of mind that allows you to see the gifts arrayed before you.

Chapter 9

Making Choices

Wiping the Slate Clean

B elieve me, I've heard it all before: "You're not smart enough." "You're not good enough." "They don't like you." "That's a stupid way of thinking; people aren't going to support that idea." "That's too hard for you to learn." "You weren't meant to be in that profession." "Time is not on your side, you'll never make it."

I didn't know the truth of who I was until I stepped out of the chaos that I created in my head and into unknown possibility. That required full and unconditional surrender to the voice that was calling me forth. The voice spoke to me through my ancestors. It spoke through the great avatars. It spoke through my teachers. The voice was not concerned with old thoughts and paradigms conditioned by the past. Ultimately, I came to know this voice to be my own: The voice that never fades. It's forever downloading the Universal goodness that is everywhere, all the time.

But it's a moment-by-moment choice to look for all the ways in which our lives are enriched by following the voice of Spirit. It's also a choice to have the courage to walk the path in faith, knowing that by doing so everything that you need on the journey will be provided.

Any situation that comes your way is an opportunity to get still and stop the chatter for a moment. While all situations can be useful, the bad situations have within them the seeds for especially powerful blessings. Crises come in different forms. Some people have been in crisis for a long time. However, I'd like to offer the idea that whatever the crisis, it's come to help the individual move to the next stage of their evolution. Even if you've lost everything, can you stop grieving long enough to picture a clean slate?

You can actually do this as an exercise if you want to. Get a pen and paper. Put your name at the top of the paper, and then list everything that you have that's important to you—the family heirlooms worth X amount of dollars, your BMW X5, your two dogs, your home, the ring on your finger, the necklace your girlfriend gave you—and on and on. Now erase or scratch out everything.

What do you have? A clean slate. How does that make you feel? Happy? Sad? Frightened? Relieved? What can you do with a clean slate? Start all over again. Instead of looking at the slate and saying, "It's empty and I have nothing," you can make the conscious choice to look at the clean slate and say, "It is empty. What would it look like to create my life anew?"

Walking Through Fear and Reclaiming Your Power

In order to be resilient enough to do this, the victim mode has to decrease. The menacing thoughts that come to blame others for your present situation must be hushed. In order to face any situation of loss in this way requires declaring your decision to take power over the circumstances. If you're facing hardship from a victimhood mind-set, it's possible to come out of the mire by honestly looking at yourself and your life and asking yourself when it was that you gave your power away. Not who you gave it to—because we've all given our power away at points in our lives to many different things and people and events.

Remembering who you gave the power away to is much less important than remembering when and why you gave it away. The actors in the play will change, but the lessons will continue to arise again and again until you face them squarely and choose to do something different. Then, when those times and situations present themselves again, you can make a different choice. If you want your power back, you can have it back. It's going to take some work, and the work cannot happen from the exterior, in other words, trying to change other people. It must come from within.

There's a very visceral fear in the average individual of losing all that they have. At its core, this is a fear of being annihilated. When people identify themselves with their ego and their personality, they tend to identify the self with their things. When they lose the things, the fear is that they will also lose the self.

Sometimes you have to simply take a chance and choose to do a new thing, even if there is a possibility of losing what you think you already have. It's an act of faith to listen to the voice that draws you forward into uncertainty, knowing that no matter what happens, you'll be provided for and something new will open up for you. Your faith tells you that wherever you land will be okay. It tells you that everything that's for you will not necessarily look like what you thought it would—but if you can stay open, you might find something that's much better than you'd ever imagined.

Again, I can only speak about that which I've experienced firsthand. I've lost everything and been homeless before. I remember going to my bank one night and seeing that my account balance was -$285. I was getting ready to perform my one-man show in a plethora of schools, which would bring in money. But I was also holding a burning vision to record a CD, which was budgeted to cost nearly $40,000. On top of that was the more present concern of the $850 in rent that was due. After my heady, financially flush days on Broadway, being in this position was incredibly humbling—and scary.

Not knowing where else to turn, I went to church to pray. At one point, I looked in my wallet and I saw that I had a little money in there. I heard the voice say, "Give it."

My first thought was, *Wait a minute! I have to spend money on groceries and fill my car up with gas...*

Spirit said, "Give to the place where you're getting the life from. What does coming here do for you?"

I thought to myself, *I couldn't live without it.*

"Okay. There you go."

"Fine," I said. "How much should I give? Ten, twenty dollars?"

"Stretch yourself."

"Look, now you're going too far. I am not going to stretch myself!"

"Okay. That's fine, too."

But I did it. I made the incredibly uncomfortable decision to stretch myself. I chose faith over fear in that moment. And what I learned was that supporting places where we get our strength from, where we plug into, is another way of supporting ourselves. Whatever we give cannot help but come back to us many times over. Whether we find ourselves in churches, synagogues, mosques, temples, study groups, or healing circles, when people join together in unconditional love, the powerful source that's in all of us is rejuvenated. That night, my faith was indeed rejuvenated and I felt as though I'd been given a powerful gift. The circumstances hadn't changed—but I had.

Shortly after that evening in church, I lost my apartment. Because I was too prideful to tell any of my friends what had happened, I ended up living in my car for a period of time. As difficult as that time was, it was also a tremendous lesson. Although self-sufficiency had always been a part of my intention, I understood clearly that no matter what I might be going through at the moment, every single thing was aligning for my good. There wasn't trial or test that could ever match up to what the Universe was calling me to do and be. Even in the midst of hardship, I heard the voice of the divine whispering in my ear that I would always be taken care of. And I believed it.

There's nothing that can come into the human experience that we don't have the resources to handle. Because there's always something greater within waiting to emerge at just those moments, if we would but trust and let it happen.

Making the Choice to Heal: Money Matters

Great healing has the potential to be created from great challenge. When you accept help with your burdens, it's an opportunity to allow life, in human form, to minister to itself. And what happens then? People cry. They laugh. They rejoice and release. They make agreements and set intentions to become more themselves. Givers and receivers both walk with renewed faith. Their minds and spirits get transformed and invigorated. You can't pay for that. There's no object or toy worth that.

That's life.

The virtue of goodness is plentiful and will always surround us with its abundance. You are automatically basking in abundance when you're in alignment with your purpose. Money can't help but be drawn into that joyful vibration. But it's a by-product of the greater mission. When people think that the opposite is true, that you make money and maybe, hopefully, enjoy yourself and give something to someone else along the way, they've got it backward. That's the tail wagging the dog.

While contemplating these things during the time when I found myself homeless, I realized that I was being called to continue to give, even though it appeared that I had nothing. The voice was letting me know that what I had to give was so much more than anyone could put a monetary value on. That revelation changed my life. I came up with brand-new goals for myself, something I call my Impossible Six—six seemingly impossible goals to be worked toward for the betterment of the planet, with the understanding that these goals are not only possible, but that they will be achieved. Whether they are achieved by me and my generation or future generations is irrelevant. The important thing is knowing that there's a goal bigger than my little self, and I'm doing something meaningful to attain it.

Working on my Impossible Six opened up new vistas of possibility that left me giddy with excitement. I never felt as abundant as I did when my attention and time were focused on being part of the force that was bringing these goals to fruition. And, slowly but surely, my external circumstances began to mirror my internal joy and wealth.

Making the Choice to Heal: Rebuilding the Self

We can all create impossible goals for ourselves with the good of the world in mind, and then have the privilege of living in joyous expectancy of their fulfillment. One of my goals is that all children have clean water to drink and bathe in everywhere on the planet. Another is that women feel safe all the time—there's no more mention of domestic violence in our society. As a matter of fact, I wish that we could all live in harmony with an absence of violence.

Another wish is that men everywhere would hold on to and appreciate their sensitivity, not only when dealing with others, but also when dealing with themselves. So I took it on as a personal endeavor to assist young men in disengaging themselves from the negative cultural codes that encourage them to use sexual conquest as a means of validating themselves. Within this way of being lies a sadness that, through time, further separates the individual from the truth of who he is. It discourages him from engaging his emotions, higher consciousness, and ability to show self-respect.

When counseling these young men, or anyone living in such self-destructive patterns, I don't condemn them. Instead, I acknowledge the potential of greatness and lotus of brilliance that we all carry. People don't thrive when they are condemned and judged. If they're doing wrong, somewhere inside they already know it and are more than likely already judging themselves more harshly than any outside force ever could. What people really crave is the knowing that, no matter what has happened in their lives, there's a way out—a way to be better.

I noticed that while I prayed and meditated on these wonderful virtues for others to embrace, I became aware of opportunities for me to engage and embody them as well. Memories, the good, the bad, and the awful, also came swirling back to me. The voice of my awakening spirit spoke to me about the situations I'd encountered in the past, and the ways in which I responded to those situations. I saw how I allowed the situations to alter my perceptions about life and myself. Sometimes these alterations were for the better. Quite often, I let circumstances draw me away from the truth of who I was—my own lotus of brilliance.

It's not easy to let go and detach from those things that have found ways to infiltrate our thoughts and our modes of seeing and being in the world. However, the path to disengaging the chatter starts with first realizing that these radicals enter from the outside. They absolutely are not inherent within our spirits. As we access the voice at the core of our being, the voice that guides us from self-destruction to self-respect, self-worth, and transformation, then we can find the proper place to put those outside, long-winded voices of separation.

The voice that matters doesn't keep the voices from coming back. Those free-flowing "taunters" will likely show up many times during your journey here. Conversely, as we give full sway to the voice of our higher self, they can no longer hang around indefinitely to torment us. Instead, those voices serve in our growth as tuning forks, allowing us the opportunity to awaken to a higher call. At our best, we're instruments of compassion and giving everywhere we go.

Let's sit and breathe and ask ourselves, "Where, and in what capacity, am I to serve and to share and to give?" Quite often the people that don't have a lot are those who know how to share, because they know what it's like to go without. Deprivation has taught them compassion. To be sure, there's a balance to be found between listening to the voice that's calling you to give of your talents and keeping your structures sound. It's harder to help someone else when your lights are out and you're walking to work because your car has been repossessed.

But there's no way around the fact that giving is key to any lasting understanding of personal success. I'm not talking about giving everything that you have because of a personal inability to receive. Some people give because they don't think that they're worth anything. They think that the person to whom they're giving deserves much more than they do. But there's no balance in that. The question to ask of the voice in that situation is, Why do I not recognize my self worth? Then you allow the answers that come forth to begin to shape a new path for yourself toward healing.

It's not wise to give from a place of lack. The goal is to give from a place where we can feel as though we're participating not only in the evolution of our own soul, but also the advancement of the hearts, minds, and souls of others.

What we don't realize is that even though we may feel like dangling participles, we've actually been put into place perfectly so that somebody else can get an opportunity to share what they have and we can have the opportunity to share what we have. It's yet another way of stepping into the divine flow. Grace allows us to contribute even when we don't think we want to. Our higher consciousness, our voice, aligns us with these opportunities to learn and grow.

When people call forth their desire to be real estate moguls or great architects or singers, they're aware that they're making a conscious choice to reach toward a goal that will greatly enhance their sense of self. However, there's something inside of us that calls things into existence under all circumstances, big and small, whether we're conscious of it or not.

Whatever is called forth can ultimately be used as a tool for the growth, and pruning, of our soul—as long as we make the choice to see it as such.

Understanding the Difference Between Taking Control and Taking Power

When you listen to the voice of love within you that directs you to follow your heart and your unique path, you'll find your outside world aligning to match how you feel about yourself. You'll find yourself saying and doing things that line up with what you really want to experience in life.

If you want to be a dancer, and yet all you hang around is football players, there's a great likelihood of being led into the athletic world. But there's a shift of consciousness that occurs when you say, "I want to take power over my life." Not control, mind you, but power. With that type of shift, you'll find yourself altering your friends and your environment to be in alignment with what you truly want. If that means that you need to be by yourself for a while, then so be it. These are the early steps and lord knows they're not always easy. But the steps are there to facilitate ever-deeper levels of awakening.

When you let go of trying to control your life and agree to take power over your life, the change is unbelievable. Understand that we can't control anything. We cannot control our thoughts, because our thoughts are going to come whether we want them to or not. We can, however, have power over our thoughts.

People try to control their lives, their thoughts, their friends, even their children. A parent of a teenage girl may think, *Well, if I tell her about all the dangers of having sex before she gets married, it will stop her from doing anything I don't want her to do.* However, as any parent will tell you, that's not necessarily true. Though a mother and father may try to control their daughter's actions, they cannot. What you do have power over is what you tell her, the instructions that you give her, and how all of this is demonstrated in your life. You can say, "You know, I made mistakes when I was younger that I'm not proud of. I got in with the wrong people. Thank goodness I turned out great. I have a wonderful family that I am grateful for. But I will tell you some things that I experienced. And I know that what I've experienced has brought me to this point, but you don't have to experience the same things if you don't want to. That's your choice."

When you give people choices, you give people power. You take away their power, and ultimately your own, when you try to exert control forcefully. When a person asks another person to do something (or not do something), there's a trust that they will do what is asked out of respect. But when people try to control the actions of another, somewhere inside, they don't believe that their needs will be respected. I would go one step farther and ask someone in this dynamic, "Do you trust and respect yourself?" Because if you do, you'll have much more comfort in the idea that others will, too. If not, other people will pick up on that and begin to treat you the same way you treat yourself.

There are people who don't believe they should be enjoying their gifts and participating fully in the world. The tormenting voice is quick to jump into their conversation and say, "Oh, this is wonderful. It must be too good to be true." Or it'll say, "I'm not going to try to do that. It probably won't work, and then I'll look stupid." It can be hard to believe in the possibility of living out the desires of the heart in one's day-to-day lives. Such a person might say something like, "I love horses. Horse riding is my passion in life. But I'll never make a living at riding horses, so I'm just going to listen to my father and become a banker." Or, like one of my panicked friends from college said to me just days before commencement service, "Charles, I don't know what I am going to do. I have a degree in history, and I have no idea what to do with it."

"I thought you were going to law school to become a lawyer, Lucy," I responded.

"I know," she sobbed with her face buried in her hands. "But that's what my parents want me to do."

Allowing other people's thoughts and plans to dictate the action of your life is not acceptable anymore once you agree to take charge of your life. It sometimes takes great courage to reconnect with your passions in a meaningful way and recognize that the thing that brings the most joy in your life is the gift that you're here to share with the world.

It sounds very simple, but being able to accept your gift in its fullness begins with first allowing yourself to recognize that you have a gift to give. There are so many people walking around the world saying, "I don't know what to do with my life. I want to live a meaningful life, but I don't know where to start. Right now I just feel like I'm getting by." But every single one of us has experienced a moment of joy, a moment of surrender, peace, and total attention when time just flew by without us even being aware of it. Think back to what you were doing during those times. Entertain the possibility that your voice was speaking to you at those moments, whether you were reading a book, climbing a mountain, or rocking a child to sleep. The voice speaks to you in your joy and tells you that this is it. This is your gift. Right here.

In life, we all have things that we're not so sure about. But it's more beneficial to choose the unknown than try to guess what may happen in the future based on what's already happened in the past. Contrary to what most people believe, the past can be a notoriously unreliable indicator of things yet to come.

While no one can force you to participate, life is offering you the opportunity to participate day by day, minute by minute, second by second. Getting out of our heads and away from the chatter helps this process, as well as acting from a place of spontaneity. When we get out of our heads, it allows the space for divine synchronicity to work on our behalf.

The call to participate in the flow of life comes to us every day in innumerable ways. It's present in all of our daily interactions, everything from giving a person a silent blessing, to giving your jacket to someone who's cold, to giving the world your talent to sing, to giving your gift to heal and protect people as a doctor or a fireman. Life admonishes us to give without being overly concerned with what we're receiving in return. We take charge of our lives by giving free reign to our desire to live and love fearlessly. We don't hold others hostage or try to take control over their behavior by playing the tit-for-tat game of "I did this for you and—if you loved me—you'd do the that for me." When we reach out and participate fully in life, the understanding arises that the place we're giving from is an inexhaustible wellspring provided by our source. No human being can give that to us and, likewise, no one can take it away. Through the universal law of reciprocity, abundance then flows into our lives with grace. We no longer have to try to manipulate or hoard, for fear of not having enough. Opportunities to receive your good come forth in ways that you could never have predicted.

For many, that concept is easy to think about but difficult to put into action. However, it's very possible to practice your giving in tangible ways. By doing so, you increase your ability to give until it becomes a second-nature way of being in the world.

Sharing Your Gifts, Sharing Yourself

When I began to step out farther, repeatedly making the choice to trust the voice, I began to feel like I wasn't alone here. Of course, I could look around and see that I wasn't the only person on the planet. But internally, the sense of isolation can be an overwhelming perception. The realization came that I'm part of a greater force in the world and, whether or not I want to take responsibility for it, what I say and what I do really affects other people.

At every opportunity where I might have normally said, "No, that's mine and I want it all," I made it a point to share whatever it was that I had.

I chose to start with what felt like a really small thing. When I was working on *The Lion King,* I bought a dozen donuts before the matinee one Sunday afternoon and took the donuts to everybody's dressing room and offered them one. Then I thought, *If I don't get one, how will I feel?* And to be honest, when I first started doing it, if everybody took one and there wasn't a donut left for me, I'd get upset.

"Oh, hell no," I'd pout. "Y'all ain't gon' eat up all my donuts!"

Then one time, after doing this exercise for a while, I passed around the donuts, and when I looked in the box I saw that every single donut had been taken. But instead of getting annoyed or feeling like I'd missed out on something, I felt nothing but joy, knowing that everybody got one … and I did, too. I just didn't eat mine. It was divine. I knew that I had stepped over the threshold, where I'd been trained to think, "I always have to have something for me!"

You don't have to start from billionaire status to give meaningfully. You can start wherever you're at in your life right now. Life is waiting to unfold for you right now. You may feel like you have no hope, nothing to give. You may feel like you no longer want to be on this earth for whatever reason. But all of that can change in the instant that you become willing to accept the change. You're one with life, and life is ready to roll out the red carpet for you.

To accept a new beginning for your life is your choice. If you're willing to be open and listen to the voice even when you have no idea what it's talking about, if you're willing to say, "I want to know," then what you ask for will show up. Not only will it show up, it'll transform your life. You have the opportunity to participate in that.

There's a party going on all the time. If you choose to come to the party, and dance, then you'll experience the oneness and the joy of the dance. But if you choose not to come, or to come to the party and stand against the wall, everything is going to continue to happen right in front of you. Don't think for a moment that if you don't show up it won't happen.

Life goes on. It's not waiting for you to show up. It's simply, lovingly allowing you the opportunity to play.

Exercise

Become silent and focus on your breathing. Then bring into mind one thought or wish for the greater good of the planet and world in which we live. As you visualize this thought, see it become fully materialized. See yourself participating in the unfolding of this wish coming to fruition. Perhaps you'd like to create something wonderful for your family, your community, and your nation. See the full transformation, the full completion of what you've created in your mind. Most important, begin to notice how you're actively participating in this thought becoming a reality.

Chapter 10

Putting It to Practice

Be the Change

One of the questions I'm often asked (and have asked myself) is: How do I continue to participate in this beautiful, yet unpredictable game of Life when things so often appear to be the opposite of the good I affirm every morning? When the bank account continues to spiral downward, when the house is in danger of foreclosure, when we turn on the television and are bombarded with stories about crime, war, poverty, and so on, how do we continue to know the best about life and about ourselves? Gandhi's mandate to be the change that we desire to see in the world has never been more poignant than it is today.

Being peace ... Being love ... Being joy ... Being harmony ... This means not just giving lip service to these virtues, but actively participating in their unfolding. The question is whether we're ready to embody what we want to see. Are we willing to put into practice those things that will elevate our planet to a higher vibration and create a world that works for everybody? That sounds pretty remarkable. It's a great concept, but it's easier said than done.

So where do we start?

At each turn of spiritual maturity is a mirror to see your unfolding life from a different perspective. This opportunity to grow in wisdom is often accompanied by people, places, and things that make us uncomfortable and, at times, fearful. Some call them challenges. Others call them roadblocks. And I'm sure you've heard people refer to them as the unholy guiles of the devil. But no matter what we call them, these seeming obstacles are actually stepping-stones to a greater awareness and, therefore, a more fulfilling life. These tuning forks allow us to hear the beautiful melody being broadcast from a Universal intelligence that has a supply of goodness for us all.

Of course, these promotions in consciousness don't come without work—internal preparation and targeted external action. Without it, our potential can never be fully realized. However, once we say, yes to doing the work, we authorize life to carry us forward in its magnificent way. This yes is not so that you can be emotionally pacified. Saying yes brings with it a kinetic energy, one that is ready to put the intention into practice. The yes initiates a dance that whisks you into a higher vibration, encouraging you to face your fears and come to know more of the truth of who and what you are.

Living the Life I Sing About

It was December 19, 2008, and Christmas was just around the corner. I was about to brave an angry northeastern wind as a winter storm bore down on New York City. I'd invited a few friends over to celebrate the season with deserts, eggnog, and cider. At 5:30 p.m. I realized that, although everything needed for the party had been purchased, nothing had been prepared. This gave me two hours to eat dinner and finish preparing before the guests arrived at 7:30 p.m.

I hustled down the street to one of my favorite Thai restaurants to grab dinner. A furious mix of snow, sleet, and rain, coupled with harsh winds, made trying to cross the street a course in skill and patience. By the time I made it to the restaurant's front door, I was covered with snow. After catching my breath, I placed my order and sat down to wait for my food. Then a friend called and I talked with him briefly on my cell phone.

During the few minutes that I chatted on my phone and waited for my order, the weather conditions grew drastically worse as temperatures continued to drop. When I stepped outside again, the sidewalks were glassy sheets that looked like the surface of an ice-skating rink. Large puddles of slush had quickly turned into small ponds extending into the streets and into the flow of traffic. Instead of stepping over them, I resorted to the track-and-field skills I used as a high school long jumper. This worked better, even though one misstep would've resulted in taking a bad tumble onto the frozen ground.

As I crossed the street, still engaged with my friend on the phone, I quickly transferred my mobile phone and the bag of food to my other hand so that I could sink my frozen fingers into my coat pocket and unthaw them. Out of habit, I felt for my belongings.

Something feels odd, I thought. *What else am I supposed to have in my pocket?* In a split second I got my answer. *Oh God, where is my wallet!?*

A feeling of panic ran through me and began to short-circuit my body. For whatever reason, one of my worst fears was to lose my wallet. Just the idea of it filled me with dread in the same way that some people have a fear of heights or suffer from claustrophobia. It was horrible. I'd felt the feeling before after misplacing my wallet in my apartment. But in my apartment, there was the consolation of knowing that it had to be within the confines of my living space—not on the streets of a storm-battered city, scattered with millions of people.

As my mind raced frantically, so did my hands, checking each pocket inside and out, nearly unstitching the jacket. But still, there was no wallet. In a panic, I hung up the phone and began to backtrack to the restaurant. My first thought was that I had left the wallet on the counter after paying the waitress for my food. I eagerly rushed through the restaurant doors.

"Did I happen to leave my wallet here? I was sitting on this corner before I left. Is there a possibility that someone may have turned it in."

"No, sir. You had your wallet with you when you left," the waitress calmly responded.

With my mind still racing, I left for another expedition through the snow-covered streets. This time I assumed a slight jog, feeling an irrational dread growing in the pit of my stomach at the thought of my wallet being gone forever. *When could I have lost it?* I wondered.

I began beating up on myself for being so careless. Cold, wet, and nauseated, I couldn't believe this was happening. I combed the area once again, my mind intent on recalling each corner at which I took a leap over a slushy pond of ice. But where could it have dropped? Once again I returned to the large intersection, and like a slug I crossed the street and stood motionless in front of a drugstore. The stress was getting the best of me. I ended up directly in front of a pharmacy. As I turned, the doors of the store opened automatically, as though to invite me in.

My head pounded from an awful tension headache. I was tempted to rush in and buy some aspirin for a quick fix, even though I almost never take over-the-counter drugs. In an attempt to ease the shooting pain in the back of my head, I closed my eyes and put my cold hands on my neck, which felt warm and almost feverish. After a few moments, I decided against getting headache medicine and instead put into practice the calming mindfulness techniques I'd learned.

In the midst of those passing by, I stood still with my eyes closed and my mind focused on the silence. In the stillness, I immediately heard the familiar, ever present voice of guidance. It gently said, "Breathe, Charles. Everything is all right. Just keep breathing. Keep noticing the breath."

I confided in the voice, surrendering my fears so I could receive its gentle direction. Finally, I relaxed into a meditative state on the busy New York City sidewalk. I visualized the air going in and out of my nostrils, filling my lungs and body. I soon felt one with the breath, and therefore everything and everyone around me. Moments later a sense of tranquility and serenity saturated my being. My mind sank into peace. After several minutes in silence, I opened my eyes and walked back to the apartment.

I called my bank and credit card companies to inform them of what happened. As I spoke to company representatives, I noticed how calm I'd become. My conversation and my words were being spoken from a place of power, knowing that every single thing was in perfect order and that I was submerged in the goodness of the Universe, despite what circumstances seemed to be showing me. During my talk with one of the bank representatives, a number appeared on the caller ID. I didn't recognize the number but immediately switched over to answer.

"Hello, is this Charles Holt?"

"Yes, this is Charles," I responded.

"This may sound strange, but I believe my producer has recovered something that belongs to you. Did you lose your wallet?"

"Yes, I did lose my wallet about an hour ago."

"Great," she said. "I'll make sure she gives you a call so that you can meet with her."

"Thank you, so much," I responded.

Less than five minutes later I received a call from the producer. She asked me a couple of questions to make sure that I was indeed the owner of the wallet. I walked to the Barnes & Noble bookstore in Union Square to meet her, and as promised she returned the wallet to me with everything intact.

After thanking her, I asked where she could have possibly found it.

"It was on the corner of 20th and 8th Avenue," she responded.

How she could have possibly spotted it under the dimly lit streetlights in a snowstorm is beyond my imagination. But she did.

"Once you found the wallet, how did you find out how to get in touch with me?" I asked. "There's not an ID card with my contact number on it in there."

It turned out that she was a theatrical director. While browsing through the contents of my wallet, she noticed my Screen Actors Guild membership card.

"I called an assistant and asked her to search your name to find a contact number for you," she said.

"Wow, what a gift, what a blessing! And on today of all days! It's my birthday today," I explained. "How can I repay you? Do I owe you anything?"

"No, thank you. It'll all come back around to me in some way," she responded. She wished me a happy birthday and disappeared into the bustling crowd of Christmas shoppers.

All the way home I tried rationalizing how, and for what reason, all this had happened. What was the possibility of a responsible individual noticing a wallet in a winter blizzard in New York City and kindly retrieving my contact information through a theatrical union (that she was familiar with because she was a director herself) so that it could be returned to me? The odds are mind-boggling. I didn't know what to attribute this birthday blessing to, other than the grace of the divine intelligence. I'm persuaded, however, that my heeding the voice and standing in the flow of peace allowed me to let go of all that would've blocked the opportunity to receive the blessing. This also allowed someone else to be blessed, since giving and receiving happen simultaneously.

My mind asked, "What if my wallet had never been returned to me?" I would've had to live with the dread of wondering if somebody had picked it up and used my cards and information for a holiday shopping spree. While wondering about this, I caught the insight: It would have been all good, no matter what.

Every single thing would have been all right, and your life would have continued to unfold in a magnificent way. The experience of your wallet leaving your possession for a while was in itself a benchmark of growth in your understanding. You continued to trust the intuitive voice and heed its instructions. You declared it so when you consciously agreed to take the breath.

During the experience of losing my wallet, admittedly one of the worst fears, I encountered the proverbial peace that passes all understanding. Having practiced the path of guided listening helped me realize that these types of events can show up for a few different reasons. One is to give us a barometer on where we are with regard to our growth. If nothing else, I learned that there's no thing, circumstance, or situation that can keep what we've come here to learn, and ultimately awaken to and embody, from us.

We're surrounded by divine goodness at all times. It waits for us to ask for its permission to show up in our lives as the light that it is. In faith, we call this energy forth—that which cannot be seen, but is revealed as the substance of our reality. Basically, we make our words become things.

Contained in this energy is love and unspeakable joy. It can fill your body with gratitude for the life that's so abundantly flowing through you. The very breath you breathe is the essence of the source of all life. It holds us all together. The stars and galaxies spin to its tune. The sun shines its rays in its presence. The very breath you take is its gift to you.

Chapter 11

The Healing Power of Forgiveness

Welcoming the Shift

There occurs a shift, or better yet a lift, in one's emotional well-being after participating in a moment of sincere forgiveness. Even your physical posture can change, too, depending on how heavy a burden you've been carrying. The weight lifts more drastically when you're the one forgiving. One of the side effects of forgiveness is a tendency toward spontaneous emotional healing. Healing brings about clarity of mind that, in turn, facilitates the expansion of the seed of brilliance within. Once this seed is activated, one has the potential to hear the voice of the higher self from an entirely new perspective.

Emotional freedom is a by-product of forgiveness, which also facilitates the space for happiness and possibility to be cultivated. The person you release through forgiveness then becomes a benefit to you in your continued expansion. In this way, life's challenges can be seen as blessings rather than struggles.

This doesn't mean, of course, that we'll go through life without experiencing pain, struggle, or fear, which people generally equate with their problems and challenges. But our awareness shifts, allowing us to consistently become conscious of our challenges as opportunities to see the truth of ourselves. Our problems become spiritual conduits that give us a bird's-eye view of what's trying to emerge through us. When we understand our challenges as blessings, we have the opportunity to say, "Oh, there's something here that's trying to get my attention. Let me stay open to seeing what it is."

However, rather than cultivate self-awareness and sincere forgiveness, the intellect will say, "Get back at them or give them a piece of your mind!" But then we get out of our higher intentions. If we say we want peace and harmony in our lives, it becomes impossible when our energy is being expended to get back at somebody. There's a misalignment there. Forgiveness is one of our most powerful tools that keeps us from getting caught up in these misalignments and, therefore, not manifesting our intentions.

I'm not trying to say that forgiveness is a magic pill that you take that instantly makes all the old hurts go away. But making a commitment to practice forgiveness and not retreating from that commitment no matter what comes up in the moment is the key to seeing your intention brought to fruition.

Forgiveness in Action

One of the most powerful testimonies about forgiveness I've ever heard in my life was the story of Gregory Bright, a man who spent 27 ½ years in prison for a murder that he didn't commit.

On October 31, 1975, 15-year-old Elliot Porter was killed in a housing project in New Orleans, Louisiana. Two assailants had shot the boy twice in the head. Gregory, who was 22 years old at the time, was brought in for questioning by the police. Gregory told the police officers that he'd been in bed asleep in his mother's apartment during the time that they said the murder took place. This didn't deter the district attorney's office from bringing second-degree murder charges against him and a second young man, who was supposed to be his accomplice. Gregory insisted that he'd never even seen the other man before, let alone committed a crime with him.

Being an indigent defendant, Gregory was assigned a court-appointed attorney who only met with him once before going to trial. The prosecutors didn't have anything in the way of physical evidence linking Gregory to the murder. What they had was the testimony of a single witness, a woman by the name of Sheila Robinson. Sheila testified that she'd been sitting in her third-floor window at 1 a.m. when she saw Gregory and his co-defendant as they appeared to be running toward something. She claimed that they ran out of her view and she then heard two gunshots. The jury only deliberated for 13 minutes before finding him guilty.

Unfortunately, the prosecutors failed to inform the jury that Sheila Robinson was a paranoid schizophrenic heroin addict who suffered from hallucinations, and whom the prosecution had paid to give her testimony. Moreover, she'd had to testify under a false name to hide her criminal history. They also didn't reveal the details of the coroner's report, which set the time of death between 7 a.m. and 8 a.m., contrary to Sheila's testimony that she heard gunshots at 1 a.m. There was also an 18-page police report in which multiple witnesses identified two other people as the shooters. Blood at the crime scene was never tested.

None of this information was admitted in open court, and Gregory Bright and his co-defendant were convicted and sentenced to life in Angola Penitentiary in Angola, Louisiana.

This would have been the end of the story if Gregory had not chosen to fight for his freedom. Encouraged by his mother, who'd stood beside him throughout the entire ordeal, Gregory began the long, arduous process of trying to clear his name. The task seemed absolutely impossible. With no attorney, the only person he had to represent him was himself. This was no small task for a young man who was illiterate, having dropped out of school in the sixth grade to care for his chronically ill stepfather who was stricken with rheumatoid arthritis.

With painstaking determination, Gregory began teaching himself to read and write. Once he'd learned to read and write, he began to teach himself the law. Once he learned enough about the law to be able to file his own briefs, Gregory Bright began the process of mounting his own appeal. It was a fight that would take more than 27 years to complete and would go all the way up to the Supreme Court.

During that time, Gregory's mother, his sole support in the world, passed away. After her death, Gregory felt like he'd lost all hope. "I felt like I was riding on four flat tires," he said of that dark time. In a fit of grief one night in his prison cell, Gregory spoke to his mother out loud and asked, "What am I going to do now? All this time, I relied on knowing that you were always there with me. You were the biggest hope that I had."

He heard his mother's voice say to him, "Regain your focus. Regain your strength and determination. I've already given you everything that you need. Now it's up to you."

It was then that Gregory knew that his mother had never left him. He also knew what he needed to do to let go of the poisonous anger that had been eating him alive for so long.

He had to forgive.

Gregory realized that he had to forgive everyone who had anything to do with the trial and his subsequent imprisonment. If he didn't, he'd be consumed by his own pain and rage to the point where he'd be unable to function, much less mount a viable defense to secure his freedom.

His unrelenting quest for wholeness and redemption finally led him to forgive the prosecutors who withheld information from the jury. He forgave the witness, Sheila Robinson. He forgave the murderers for taking an innocent life and allowing him to shoulder the blame for their crime. He forgave the warden at Angola, who regularly told the prisoners, "Y'all gonna die in here. You know that, don't you? Y'all are never going to be free." According to Gregory, there were others like him who'd been thrown in prison to rot for crimes that they hadn't committed. Most of those men literally did die in prison. Gregory had to work very hard to forgive a system that could repeatedly allow innocent lives to be thrown away.

The pivotal point came when Gregory was able to forgive himself. He forgave himself for all the ways in which he'd judged himself and for all the times he felt like giving up. He also forgave himself for being angry with his mother for abandoning him. He was finally able to see that, although she had died, she'd never left him. Through Gregory's ability to forgive, he was finally, truly set free.

In 2003, the Supreme Court exonerated Gregory Bright. But because his conscience was clear and his heart at peace, Gregory had considered himself a free man long before the state let him out of prison. When he and his co-defendant were released, they were given a $10 check and a trash bag filled with all of their legal paperwork. They were released back into society with no other form of assistance.

Gregory Bright still struggles. It's nearly impossible for him to find a job. He doesn't qualify for social security. He has no medical coverage. He hasn't received any financial compensation, as of this writing. He is entitled to receive $15,000 a year for ten years as restitution, but even that paltry sum has not made its way to him. He doesn't even qualify for reentry programs, because he's technically not a parolee.

Gregory has spent many nights sleeping in his car. But through all of that, he's remained grateful. He has his freedom. He doesn't have to ask permission to use the telephone. If he's cold, he can put a coat on without first having to clear it through someone else. His total commitment to forgiveness cleared the way for Gregory's heart to remain open and thankful, despite all of the hardships that he's endured.

I had the honor of playing Gregory Bright in a one-man show called *Never Fight a Shark in Water* in New Orleans, where he lives. I was struck by his humble wisdom and his ability to see life for the gift that it is, regardless of circumstance. Through Gregory, I was able to see that actual forgiveness isn't just forgiving someone else. It's releasing yourself to your greater good. Forgiveness is a release from bondage, from whatever prison that you've locked yourself inside.

Our Greatest Teachers

Most people don't have stories as dramatic as Gregory Bright. But the ability to forgive still plays just as important a role for all of us, regardless of what the circumstances actually look like or what we might be going through.

I was able to put my newfound understanding of forgiveness into practice during a trip home to visit my family. For six months, I stayed in Nashville, Tennessee, where I was able to be with my parents on a daily basis for the first time in years. While I was there, I'd noticed that my father had changed. Far from the harsh, judgmental man I thought I knew growing up, the man who stood before me could no longer see me without telling me that he loved me. He'd always admonish me to "be good" and "be the best at what you do" and "be careful!"

Listening to my parents speak those words to me, my initial, programmed response was to try to hold on to my anger and unforgiveness. I'd start grumbling in my mind, *I know I'm the youngest, but why y'all have to keep harping at me to be careful?*

Then Spirit spoke to me one day and said, "They speak to you that way because they know what you came here to do. They recognize who you are. Even though the words sound like they're still hovering over you and treating you like a little boy, the reality is that they understand that the gift that you came to reveal and demonstrate on this earth is so powerful that they don't want you to miss a beat on your path. They're always admonishing you to 'be careful.' But consider that what they may really be saying is 'we're championing your words!"

They express themselves the way that they do because they're using the words that they know. Human beings always, and can only, use the words that they know. So they say, "Be careful" when they could just as easily be saying, "We're sending our angels of mercy to watch over you."

I contemplated that for a long while. I realized that I still, after all this time and all the things that I'd learned, had not been able to release the past fully. I'd been having an emotional reaction based on what I believed to be my parents' motivations based on what I thought I knew from the past. If I'd fully been able to forgive and release my emotional hurts, I wouldn't have been so quick to judge them or feel aggrieved by their well-meaning comments.

Part of forgiveness is being able to release the past and all that we believe that we know.

This allows us to switch off from being the victim and being tied to all the negative thoughts and meanings that we've conjured in our minds over the years. I was able to release the beliefs that I'd held that said, "My father never liked me. He was jealous of me. He hated me. He didn't like for his friends to say anything good about me."

These are all of the stories that I had made up in my mind about my father.

However, as I contemplated this revelation, Spirit spoke to me again and said, "Your father was your greatest teacher."

"How so?" I asked.

"Because he came here and loved you from this place which was painful for him. Don't you think it was hard for him to say the hurtful things that he said? Did you ever stop to think that maybe that's what his father had told him? It may have gotten across to him, which was how he learned to use those particular words, but it was still painful. You cannot project your idea of how you think people should speak to you onto somebody else."

Having fully forgiven my father, I now realize just how much of an incredible blessing he's been in my life. I'd asked for him and his teachings. Whoever crosses your path gives you the opportunity to ask the question, "Why is this experience here? What can I learn now?"

When the warden in Angola Penitentiary would tell the prisoners, "All y'all gonna die in here!" Gregory Bright had the presence of mind to say to himself, "He's not talking about me!" There's a freedom in that energy, because it doesn't latch onto whatever the ego is trying to conjure up to get back at the warden, someone who'd purposely try to crush the spirit of another living being. The ego always wants to be right, and it always wants to have the last word. But if there's nothing for the ego to latch onto in the communication, there's no need to become immersed in that negative energy.

For most of my life, I'd seen my father as cold and disapproving. However, it was only after I was able to approach him with total forgiveness in my heart (and ultimately participate in our reconciliation) that I was able to see how my own unforgiveness had stymied me in my life. Once I allowed forgiveness to enter my heart, my life took off in ways that I could never have imagined. Over time I came to realize that Spirit was absolutely right! My father was my greatest teacher. There were so many gifts and blessings that my father bestowed upon me through our interactions over the years, whether I recognized them at the time or not.

As I contemplated this, I wondered if it had been part of my father's spiritual responsibility to put those "obstacles" along my course. Had the lessons I learned actually helped me develop as a happy young man and mature human being? If this was the case, my father was really never a hindrance or obstacle. He was fulfilling his mission in being a part of my unfolding. This was somewhat difficult to make sense of at first. It didn't sound fair or logical at all.

A spiritual revolution took place in my own soul the day I forgave my father. Breaking those chains not only freed him, but it freed me as well, and perhaps even the generations that came before us. I'd been imprisoned for most of my life in my own conscious mind. The bars that held me were built from misinterpreted stories I'd made to be real in my head.

Forgiveness is vital in preparing us for the next step in our evolution, as we become more of the truth of who we are. People often allow what they believe are the facts of a given situation to weigh too heavily in their minds, giving the intellect permission to interfere with the affairs of our intuitive nature and higher intention. This behavior seems to be normal, because we practice it over and over again. It creates a standard for us to criticize and judge everything and everybody based on assumptions and exterior motives. If I think that somebody or something is wrong, it's therefore much easier to blame them for any unpleasantness that I experience in my day-to-day life.

However, when we set the intention as to get to the truth of the matter, to actually question the facts, statistics, or other exterior markers, a new opportunity presents itself. It's the opportunity to move into a higher consciousness that has less to do with pointing the finger of blame and more to do with being interested in understanding and embracing the totality of our life experience.

Forgiveness is a necessary and important process. And it's not the final course of action. I've now learned to see beyond forgiveness, that there's yet another hidden treasure to be discovered. In the process of forgiving my father, I began to understand the many dimensions of expanding awareness that I was now privy to experiencing. My relationship with my father (or the seeming lack of relationship) was a blessing in disguise, because once I began to focus my attention on better understanding him, I was able to see past my own selfishness. This shift allowed enough light to shine on the situation that I could finally dissolve the shadows of misunderstanding, which had been holding me prisoner in so many areas of life.

It doesn't matter what a situation looks like or what it sounds like. There's really nothing and no one to fear. There's only a lack of light we project on whatever we're facing. When we blame people and situations for not being what we want them to be, rather than accepting them for exactly what they are, we miss the diamond buried inside the lump of coal—the opportunity to expand our awareness and choose differently.

As we choose to change our minds and open up to possibilities, the seemingly bad or evil events of our lives will begin to dissolve. The flow of heightened consciousness that creates the dissolution is anchored in an unshakable knowing that no person, word, or deed can hurt, damage, or endanger us. Who we truly are is so much greater than any physical circumstance, and will outlast every circumstance up to, and including, death itself.

Will questions remain? Sure they will. We may never know the full scope of a situation or get detailed answers to our inquiries. We may never get closure or the apology that we deserve. Those who've committed acts of violence against us may never face justice publically. Sometimes these things happen in life. However, one can rest in the truth that if an answer goes unrevealed, its still possible to count it as a blessing. After all, we're here with another opportunity to change our minds and our ways of being. What matters most is knowing that whatever we experience shows up to allow us to shed our layers so that we may shine our light on the world.

As the muscle of conscious awareness becomes stronger through practice, the movement toward self-realization and the personal spiritual mandate can expand. I am sure that you have somebody who comes to mind in your forgiveness realm. The thought of this person may be hidden under months or years of mental debris. Maybe it was a first grade teacher or the person yesterday at the checkout counter. Could it possibly be a former best friend or a sibling?

In forgiving that person, is it possible for you to forgive yourself, too? Can you let go of all the blame associated with what you did "wrong" and celebrate what you got right?

I'd say that's a real good place to start.

Chapter 12

The Beauty of Release

Becoming a Conduit for the Divine

F orgiveness is not the only area of our spiritual journey where the ability to release what no longer serves us becomes of paramount importance. In order to grow into a higher purpose, in order to allow Spirit to flow through us so freely that we become a conduit for the divine, we must release limiting thoughts and agendas that would hinder this interaction.

I first began to fully grasp the idea of being a spiritual conduit one summer as I toured centers and churches across the country. I remember walking to my car after a Sunday-morning service in Tustin, California, where I was guest vocalist. A small-framed Latina woman stopped me just as I stepped from the sidewalk.

"While you were singing this morning, something happened in my body," she said. "Something shifted. I know that I was healed. I know that a physical healing occurred in my body."

Tears of gratitude welled up in her eyes.

"What did you feel?" I asked.

"I can't explain it—I just can't explain it," she replied.

I saw the magnitude of what she'd experienced in her eyes as she searched for the right words. However, at that time I had little more than a vague understanding of what the woman was actually trying to articulate.

As long as I'd been singing, people had always encouraged and admonished me to use the gift for a higher purpose than to simply entertain. I'd heard time and again, "Baby, whatever you do, don't you ever stop singing! You got healing power in those vocal chords."

I didn't always understand the gift of song until I finally asked myself why I felt like I was being physically lifted while listening to Donny Hathaway, Marvin Gaye, Stevie Wonder, and Aretha Franklin sing. What was so special and transformative about these people and their music? I remember watching my friend Carl Anderson onstage, singing "Heaven on Their Minds" in *Jesus Christ Superstar* and noticing how he seemed to be taken over by some unknown force during the course of the song. It wasn't just his marvelous way of playing his character, Judas. No, it was much more.

It was as if his entire body had been taken over by an unseen energy. I remember watching him on stage thinking, *He's gone.* And gone he was. He hadn't physically left the space. But he'd moved just far enough out of the way for whatever it was that had taken over to use him as a vessel, a conduit to show its glorious face.

"Could this be what's happening with me now?" I asked myself.

As each Sunday rolled by, I found myself releasing more of Charles, and allowing more of that glorious energy to have its way.

This energy continued to grow the more I performed. During one show the following spring, I felt the most incredible surge rush through me that I'd ever experienced in my life. I felt as if I was going to take flight and, with outstretched arms, go soaring out of the building. After I finished the song—or quite frankly, after the song finished me—I returned to my seat. I was too electrified to ask myself what had happened. All I knew was that whatever I'd witnessed moving through Carl had just coursed through me.

I suddenly realized that neither my life nor the way I sang would ever be the same after that experience. What had brought about this wonderful yet overwhelming feeling of enlightenment? The one word that kept coming to mind was *yes*.

"What does yes have to do with what just happened?" I wondered.

Before I could search for the answer, the voice gently reminded me that I'd said yes to the will of the divine unfolding as my life. Not only had I said yes, I'd also increased my level of participation. Somewhere in all of my repetitive and fervent personal pleas for God to use me, I'd unknowingly stepped into the next stage of surrender. It happened without regard to details or how I thought things were supposed to look. I'd been too emotionally tired to try and fix or manipulate the situations in my life. In earnest I'd said, "Okay, God, I'll do what it is that you want of me."

With no more questions asked, I released my need to control outcomes and trusted that I'd be used as a vessel to manifest the face of unconditional love. I surrendered myself so that other people's lives could be lifted to a higher vibration of healing, joy, and freedom. *Use me*, I'd prayed. I'd wanted this more than any thing in the world. But before this could occur, I also had to release my preconceived notions of what surrender and being used for a higher purpose should look like. I continued to do the inner work: meditating, sitting in focused silence, praying, and sharing my gifts and talents.

When ingrained thoughts and habits are released, your true intention lines up with a higher vibration. Giving up things that no longer serve your evolution is necessary to become a clearer channel or vessel. A new foundation of elevated awareness is constructed and put into its proper place as the bedrock that undergirds the creation of your life. The slate is wiped clean and ready for you to create an entirely new landscape.

When you have a soul-moving experience like this, it can cause a shift so profound and pattern shattering that you feel as if you've been covered in a new body as well. All things seem fresh and exciting and full of possibility, because the table has been set for all things to become new through the act of your unconditional surrender.

Take a deep breath.

Feel the air rush in and out of your lungs, coursing through your entire body. Notice how easily your body accepts the life-giving force of this breath. There's no resistance. There's no strife. There's no anxiety or frantic anticipation. The body has found its place in allowing the breath of life to breathe through it. It has surrendered. Just as the body goes through this process, so does the spirit within you knows that in order for you to fulfill the purpose you've come here with, you must surrender to that purpose.

In this feeling tone, allow yourself to contemplate what it would feel like to give up on having your agenda and needs met. What would it feel like to give in to allowing the brilliance inside you to connect with the higher call of the universal intelligence? When we say yes, when we consciously connect to the source of all that exists through our willingness, we set the stage for our greater unfolding.

Continue to breath and say yes to the surrender.

Detachment: Letting It All Go in Order to Grow

Throughout the majority of my life, I contended with the part of me that felt it had to win at all costs, whether in word or deed. I was never without a plan B that (according to my ego) would surely put me on top. The mental garbage that I'd accumulated during my life was evidence of my unwillingness to let go of this idea, along with others like it. This was true even though the thoughts, words, and actions that I held on to from the past were in direct contradiction to the truths I'd learned and was attempting to put into practice in the present.

As a person journeys through life, there are certain things he or she picks up along the way: beliefs, ideas, personality traits, sensitivities, attitudes, etc. Whether we deem them good or bad, these ways of being ultimately serve us in our growth. However, for most people, the tricky part is learning how and when to let go of the beliefs and habits that have outlived their usefulness. Even though my desire to always win was crippling to my spiritual growth, for the longest time I had no idea how to let go of that way of being. It had been ingrained in me after so many years of proving myself through competition.

Then one day while sitting in meditation, I had an epiphany about the power of detachment and letting go.

I saw myself as a child of four sitting in church with my mother, listening to the pastor as he gave a sermon on eagles. Reverend S.H. Simpson was revered as one of the best preachers in the city of Nashville and the surrounding area. He was a tall, imposing man with dark skin who always wore spectacles around his somewhat pronounced eyes. This always made him look pensive, as if he was continuously in deep though about something. Reverend Simpson was known for his charismatic tone and swagger. His words were so inspiring that even the most solemn congregants would eventually be on their feet, screaming and shouting praises to God. However, the thing that struck me most about Reverend Simpson was his ability to tell a story. And, like I mentioned, on this particular day his topic was eagles.

"The mother eagle stirs in her nest," he said. "One-by-one, she begins to take each little eaglet on her wing and fly from the nest to the highest altitude."

As he spoke, I saw in my four-year-old mind the big mamma bird flying far above the trees against a clear blue sky with the baby bird clutching on for dear life.

"And when she reaches that certain height," he continued, "she releases the chick from her wing and flies away, leaving the eaglet to fly on its own."

When Reverend Simpson said this, I became extremely upset. The idea that the mother eagle would let go of her babies, leaving them alone and afraid to plummet toward the earth was terrible. Wondering if the baby chicks made it through their passage to safety, I asked my mother what she thought about the mother eagle's decision to leave the baby chicks to fly on their own.

"Son, there comes a time when you have to let go, even if it's the one thing you love most, so that it can continue to grow and experience a wonderful life."

I tried to understand what my mother was saying. But I still wasn't sure if I agreed with the mother eagle just taking off from the seemingly helpless babies. In the end, I decided to trust my mother's confident tone and explanation even if I didn't necessarily agree with her train of thought. Of course, much later, I'd realized that she understood the mother eagle's intention, and though not an easy thing for her to do, my mother had been through her own rites of passage with my brother and sister. At the time, however, letting go felt synonymous with betrayal to my young mind.

I continued to meditate while the scenario played out in my mind. But rather than being disturbed, I found myself thinking, *What a lucky little bird. It's mother was wise in knowing when to release it from her grip in order for it to fulfill its destiny, knowing that a selfish desire to keep it nearby under her protective wing would only stunt its growth and development.*

But how did the mother eagle know when it was time to let the babies go? What told her that it was time for them to fly on their own?

Intuition. Instinct.

When you trust the higher guide inside, it'll lead you deep into your intuitive wisdom. The mother bird realized in some instinctual way that her natural desire to serve and protect the young chicks could not be confused with holding on to the chicks in desperation. She had to let go in order for them to grow and in order for her to continue on her course and journey as well.

It's not easy to release people, things, or ways of being that we've grown accustomed to. Letting go can be one of the most difficult tasks to perform, and it takes a strong, yet conscious individual to fully release. Often, our willingness to release is the key that unlocks the door to the next phase of our lives. However, even when we know this, it can still be a struggle.

We just can't seem to find the door.

In most indigenous cultures, people learn to release within the context of various rites of passage, which are experienced throughout a lifetime. They release one stage of living in order to embrace the next stage. In Western culture, however, releasing is often misconstrued as losing something, rather than being a necessary part of the process of gaining something bigger and better.

Rites of Passage: The Meaning, the Beauty, and the Bliss of Release

When we experience a rite of passage, it quite often comes to us as a challenge or situation that moves us out of the life that we're used to and into a new way of being. However, standing between the old and the new will generally be some sort of trial or obstacle that tests our fortitude. In reality, the obstacle is really an opportunity for us to learn more about life and ourselves in the process of overcoming the challenge. The rite of passage symbolizes our willingness to trust and surrender to our own soul's development.

The word *passage* literally speaks to something that is passing through our experience. Unfortunately, some people, in their unwillingness to let go of what they already know, only see the obstacle part of the rite of passage. They pay little attention to new phase of development that they are moving into.

For example, being released from a job can be seen as a rite of passage. A person who has been fired is releasing one stage of being in life while (hopefully) becoming aware that they're standing on the precipice of something that has the potential to be much greater. Juxtapose that line of thinking with the line of thinking that says, "Oh, great! I just got fired!"

The connotation behind getting fired is usually negative. No one likes to be fired. The feeling tone behind being fired says that you weren't doing a good job or that you weren't liked on your job—specifically the boss didn't like you. These things may or may not be true. But looking at it the other way allows for the acknowledgment that there's something exciting taking place beyond simply being released from a job. The focus then goes directly to: What else is possible for me?

In seeing life's inevitable changes as rites of passage rather than crises, we have the opportunity to look at the potential behind these situations differently. We can choose not to feel like we're inadequate or a victim of someone else's judgment about us. Quite often, there's a great reluctance surrounding change of any sort. Using the example of being fired, a person may hate his job and constantly dream of leaving, but the minute he's fired, there arises a feeling that says, "No, I don't want to go. You're making me go!" This struggle doesn't serve either side: the person being released or the one doing the releasing.

But trusting the process of release allows the employee to say, "Once I let go of this job, I know that something greater is going to come into my life to take its place." This is how passage takes on the energy of willingness, allowing what has transpired in our lives to make its way through our experience without struggle.

Once the mind sees another option of looking at something, it gives us the opportunity to exhale and release gently, with gratitude rather than fear. Even the body temple knows that the inhalation of breath must be followed by the exhalation, or release, of that same breath. The body temple doesn't fight to maintain the breath that it already has. It doesn't ask permission to take another breath. It simply breathes. Such is life. When we continue to breathe easily and freely, embracing the different passages as they flow through our lives, then whatever is trying to emerge will give us everything we need to move through the period of transition.

That is what rites of passage are for: giving us a context with which to see change as a blessing and a gain, rather than a loss. We come to understand release as a wonderful and necessary component of life, rather than something to be resisted and shunned. It becomes apparent that the process of letting go has the power and potential to generate life energy for everybody: the one who's releasing and the one who's being released.

The opposite happens when you hang on and resist the shift. You entangle others in your web of confusion and become victim of your own attachment. You can easily justify being stuck by using what happened in the past, good or bad, as the standard by which you judge what's possible for the future. Whether we release by choice or by force, the lessons learned are much more valuable than anything we perceive to be lost.

Don't believe me?

Try this exercise: Sit up straight, with your palms facing upwards in a position of receptivity. Inhale deeply. As you inhale, bring into mind all that you wish to release—those things that seem to weigh you down, those negative words that have followed you for so long and have thwarted your confidence, those people who you've held captive in your mind and heart. Bring all of this into your awareness with the intention of letting it all go. You may choose to focus or concentrate on one of these things or people. You may choose to focus on them all. Now exhale.

As you exhale, see this negative energy leave your body, fading from your consciousness like hot steam into the air. Repeat this conscious inhalation and exhalation as many times as necessary until you begin to feel lighter. Take a few moments to stay in the silence. Now, focus your attention, and intention, on what you want to experience.

Going Over the Falls

The process of letting go and releasing can take you as far back as your childhood or to something that may have happened a few seconds ago. As you let go of mind clutter, you help clear the path for whatever is seeking to manifest itself through you. And remember—what seeks to manifest through you, endeavors to minster to you as well.

As you surrender stagnant ideas and ways of being, "floaters," as I call them, will surface. Floaters are things that need to have more love and attention given to them. Healing and forgiveness work that hasn't been completed resurfaces, bringing a person, place, or thing rushing to your mind and heart to be addressed with proper order. Though it may not feel like it, floaters don't come as hindrances, but as blessings. They help you clear out the blockages that are hampering your graduation to your next stage. They make apparent the areas in your life and relationships that require a greater commitment to forgiveness and surrender.

Surrender is essential when one seeks to become a beneficial presence on the planet. Whether it's surrendering to a better diet or surrendering to a higher spiritual practice, surrender can make the critical difference in one's spiritual, emotional, physical, and even financial unfolding. Like the process of releasing, surrender is, in part, an act of giving something up. Both processes are a course in soul-searching that, at their deepest level, require one to jump into the depths of the unknown. One must trust that he or she will be buoyed, rather than dragged down to the depths.

During meditation one morning, my higher consciousness—Spirit, as some may refer to it—requested that I stop treading water and let the flow of life carry me over the falls. Immediately, in my mind, I saw what looked like a violent rush of water as I stared from afar at Niagara Falls. I had witnessed the brilliance of this natural phenomenon while on tour with *Jesus Christ Superstar*. I remembered vividly the other members of the cast and myself staring in awe at the beauty and strength of the falls. As the voice admonished that I jump into the water, I saw myself coming closer to the falls.

"Breathe, Charles. Just take a deep breathe. There is no need to fear. I am here with you."

I jumped.

As I plunged over the falls, I noticed that the violent rush of water was not at all the monster I had, as a spectator, thought it to be. As a matter of fact, it was harmless. Indeed, the water was simply doing what it does best—flow. As I continued down the falls, I realized that this giant, natural source of energy was embracing me as a part of itself. The water and I were now one. I completely surrendered, and there came over me a dynamic feeling of unspeakable peace.

Now we're not talking in literal terms here. I wouldn't physically jump into this giant body of water, and neither should you. However, this serves as a demonstration of how we may use our imagination to become as one with what we believe the voice of truth is trying to convey to and through us. This consciousness will always speak in ways each of us can understand.

Once my meditation was over, I opened my eyes. It dawned on me that my yes was tantamount to giving permission for the presence of Spirit to work its splendor through me. Shortly after this experience, I noticed a transformation in different areas of my life. The first place where I noticed a change was in my singing. The notes I hit didn't seem any clearer. They weren't any higher or more sustained. I was singing songs I'd known and performed many times over. But something had been emphatically altered.

I noticed an ease and grace come over me whenever I sang. The words began to flow through in a sweet and delicious way. That's not to say that fear, anxiety, and frustration didn't continue to visit me on occasion. But I now understood that I had the option to fasten my thoughts and intentions on those things that lifted me higher. I could focus on the things that fed the surge, which rushed me over the falls into the flow of peace and awareness.

Once you jump in the water, the only thing left to do is swim. As any swimmer knows, it's much easier to swim with the current than it is to struggle against it. In the case of surrendering to the voice of guidance and higher consciousness, one must practice going with the flow or, in other words, releasing into nonresistance. This is the very essence of life, which we call love, peace, healing, freedom, harmony, and abundance. By allowing yourself to be available, you give the universe permission to demonstrate through you the goodness that we're all here to experience.

Chapter 13

Love: What It All Boils Down To

Freedom Is Love in Expression

Once the work behind your spiritual practice begins to bear fruit, it can also sometimes bring with it unpleasant feelings and realizations. It can be very disheartening to discover that you've been trying to "fix" yourself and "get it right" when there was never anything wrong with you to begin with. Anger, alienation, and loneliness are common feelings that people go through at this stage. It can be humiliating to feel as though people hoodwinked you by convincing you to believe things about life and yourself that are false.

But even through pain and shame, the spirit of unconditional love that allowed for the breakthroughs in the first place is still operating. It provides the means to move through anger or sadness into freedom. When you're free in the mind—free from the standpoint of not putting attachments on anything or anyone—it's bliss. This freedom is another way to open the door to your creative brilliance and excellence. If we listen with a humble, open heart, we can hear the voice saying, "I'm still here. There are still great possibilities all around you." The understanding that I get another shot at this is awesome and exhilarating. From this vantage point you, and everything else in your life, can be made new. All of these realizations hold within them the makings of a life of love.

Finding Jesus in Japan

Until I started touring as a performer, I'd never traveled very much. I'd only been out of the country once, and that was on a trip to Canada. For my first real international excursion, I was making a 23-hour, transcontinental trip to Japan for a month's tour of *Smokey Joe's Cafe*. Although I wasn't a novice at flying, I had no idea of how being on a plane for nearly the full course of a day would be. I remember sitting in the seat next to the window, nearly having an anxiety attack during the first half of the flight. I was so nervous and restless that I wanted to offer the pilot a hand at helping him fly. Pacing like a caged tiger, I found that many of the other passengers were passing the time by playing board games. But anything requiring concentration was not on my menu. The only reason for me to settle back in my seat was meal service and a quick nap.

After what felt like an eternity, we finally arrived to our destination on the other side of the world. Our first stop was in Okinawa. I'd learned a couple of basic Japanese terms before arriving, and the people I met were quite understanding and accommodating with regard to the language barrier. Taken by this new and fascinating experience, I must admit, the first week seemed like a blur. The only thing I remember is how I ate noodles each and every meal. I found them to be the only food that would fill my appetite, and the hot, steamy broth that they soaked in was absolutely delicious, reminding me of my mother's homemade chicken-noodle soup.

I immediately noticed how hospitable and generous the Japanese were, always extending themselves to make sure we were comfortable and welcomed. During the entire stay I not only felt accepted but embraced by a group of people with whom, before the visit, I had very little contact. The only thing I had to reach for was an occasional high note during the performance.

Are they on their best behavior because of us? I wondered. *Or is this a natural part of their culture?*

Whatever the case, it made me feel right at home. Our opening night in Okinawa was outstanding. We performed to a packed house full of ecstatic fans and standing ovations. After the show, we proceeded out of the theater and on to the opening-night festivities. We walked the red carpet on the way to our bus, overwhelmed by fans who were still screaming at the top of their lungs with happy tears streaming down their faces. I remembered seeing this type of behavior as I watched Michael Jackson in concert on television, but being in the midst of this joyful mayhem was overpowering.

As we left the parking lot, I looked back to find mobs of fans rushing to our bus, blowing kisses and yelling, "Come back!" and "We love you!"

They said they love us, I thought. *How is it possible to say you love somebody without really knowing them?*

For a long while, I contemplated the idea that love is one of those things that shows up in many different shapes, forms, and sizes; and how its presence could be evoked by the seemingly slightest gesture. This wasn't exactly a new thought for me, but I'd never seen this principal demonstrated in such an effusive way before.

We spent our second week in Fukuoka. The hotel we stayed in was a few blocks from the huge stadium that was home to one of Japan's top professional baseball teams, the Fukuoka Softbank Hawks. Unlike the faster-paced, concrete jungle of downtown Okinawa, Fukuoka had more of a strolling pace. I spent most of my spare time walking around, taking in the beauty of the city and its panoramic views, while exchanging kind nods with people passing by. Although Fukuoka's population exceeded 2 million, it's quaint, relaxed atmosphere suggested a city of a much more intimate size. The part of the city where we stayed was quiet with lots of green, healthy-looking trees and singing birds that seemed to be happy to be alive. There were birds in our hotel as well, living in their own designated tree-filled atrium. Again, I was struck by the feeling of warmth, generosity, and kindness that seemed to radiate from the people I encountered. To witness that level of goodwill amongst strangers affected me in a profound way.

Our final two weeks were spent in Tokyo.

Tokyo is a bustling town, to say the least. I thought New York was fast-paced and crowded. It only took me stepping off the tour bus to feel the frenetic energy whiz my head. There were masses of people everywhere I looked. Tokyo made New York seem like a quaint little Southern town. Not only did Tokyo have an overwhelming population, but it seemed to have a number of mini-cities all wrapped up into one flourishing metropolis.

Its skyline, even more dynamic than New York City's, seemed endless.

The hotel we stayed in was enormous and located within close proximity to popular attractions, including the young, trendy fashions of Harajuku and the electronics stores near the Shibuya section of Tokyo's massive sprawl. We were greeted with open arms and plenty of kind gestures. After settling my luggage and bags into my room, I immediately set my sights on getting to know the city and my surroundings. I was eager to test my navigation skills in the unfamiliar streets.

My first stop was the subway. It looked like a giant maze on paper, nearly running out of colors to distinguish the different routes and directions. As I stepped from the platform onto the train, I was reminded of my trips on the subway in New York City. Though the subway cars were noticeably cleaner, people were smashed into one another like sardines in a can. Right away, I recognized the familiar sound of the train and the rustle of passenger activity as they entered and exited. In spite of the fact that I'd never seen or experienced this many people in one place in my life, there was a calm to this swarm of inhabitants. At times, the silence on the train was deafening. It was so quiet that one really could hear a pin drop.

This was not helpful to me.

As a matter of fact, the silence made me feel uncomfortable. I became paranoid and nervous after a while.

It's too quiet, I thought. *Did I miss something? Is something about to happen that I don't know about? There's no other person on the train that looks like me. There's certainly no other person with my skin color on here.*

The chatter in my mind started getting crazy. As my eyes cautiously wandered around, I noticed the tranquil, almost meditative look on the faces of most of the people around me. Some were reading books, others the newspaper, and then there were those who, unlike me, seemed to be patiently enjoying the ride. After I finally unraveled and settled into the ride, I began to question what I was seeing in earnest. This cloud of a seemingly static energy was, in its silence, a kinetically active force.

How could being quiet and not thinking be active? I asked myself.

For the moment, no answer came.

The opening night of the show in Tokyo was magnificent! In fact, the entire two-week run felt like one long opening night celebration. Everybody from the crew to the cast settled into their respective jobs, and the respect for one another continued to grow during our stay. We enjoyed each other's company outside of the theater as well. We shopped together at exotic stores and ate at great restaurants. As nice as all of that was, there was something more poignant about the trip. As hard as I tried, I couldn't put my finger on it at first. Slowly, I began to realize that the way of being that I'd always known—my thoughts, judgments, and pre-conceived notions—were changing as a result of being in this new place.

The night before I was to return home to New York, I had a conversation with one of the stagehands who I'd befriended during my time there. He was born and raised in Tokyo and shared with me how it was growing up there. Although much of what he shared was different than my experiences growing up in the Western tradition, many things felt familiar, reminding me of my own experiences in Nashville.

As he continued talking, I suddenly realized that there was one topic that I wanted to know about more than anything else. I'd heard and read about the more reflective, respectful nature of Eastern tradition. But I wanted to find out from someone who was born into this tradition how it affected his daily life and worldview.

"Before we go any further," I said, "I have to ask you a question. You're Buddhist, aren't you?"

"Yes, I am," he gently answered.

I took this as an invitation to ask more questions, disregarding all the advice from friends who thought asking questions about one's religious beliefs to be disrespectful and unwarranted. Contrary to rule, he seemed more than willing to share. I explained my religious upbringing in great detail, and he answered every question that my eager mind could find out about his. As we exchanged stories about our religious and spiritual backgrounds, I found myself drawn to the beauty and the wisdom he described as inherent within Buddhism tradition. The more he talked, the more I wanted to know about this spiritual path and its practice.

"Common to Buddhism is the practice of meditation and the withdrawal from external objects and thoughts. This is essential as you learn how to steady the mind," he said.

Far from becoming steadier, these concepts made my mind race.

"So," I questioned, "the intention in meditation is to bring one's mind to a place of focused silence long enough so that it can become free from emotions and turmoil?"

"Basically," he replied.

The conversation continued deep into the night and then lingered in my mind long after the trip to Japan had ended. My friend's words followed me back to my New York apartment and weighed on my mind for months.

As happy as I was to be home again, there'd been a part of me that hadn't wanted to leave Japan. It felt like I was leaving a part of me behind.

"That doesn't make sense," I told myself. "My life will go on like it always has, and I'll probably never see these people again."

This train of thought was my way of hardening myself so that I wouldn't allow my emotions to get the best of me. But my feelings wouldn't let me go.

I had flashbacks of my encounters with the people in Japan. I dreamed about them and the kindness I experienced and bright smiling faces I saw in all the cities that we traveled to. I spent hours walking through Central Park while reliving these conversations and experiences. I couldn't have explained to anybody what I was feeling, for it was nothing less than a shift in my consciousness and my awareness about life—a growing awareness about myself and the perceptions that I'd long held of the those who were the "other."

Where I grew up, religion was as serious as life and death. Understanding where one stood with God was just as important as obeying one's mother and father. Grandparents and elders in the community and the church often quizzed the children on the importance of religion and its priority.

As a child, you could expect to be asked questions like: "Do you love your mother? Do you love your father? How about your brother and sister? But who do love more than anybody in the whole wide world?"

If your answer wasn't "Jesus," then you were cast aside and labeled a heathen child "bound for the pit of hell!" Prayer and fasting on your behalf was immediate and your "case" was treated like a patient who needed open-heart surgery.

The dogma that I'd grown up with became a set of guidelines by which I lived my life. I managed to be the good little Christian boy who people expected me to be. However, I was no longer a child and often felt hard-pressed to heed the principles that I now felt were forced upon me. Things were changing quickly, and my thoughts and feelings were the first to bend. The rigid standards I'd once revered as the only way to live life were coming into question.

By the time I was 22, I had been "dipped" twice, first as a Baptist, then as a Pentecostal. Whether you were Baptist or Pentecostal, the only way to receive a key to the kingdom of heaven was to be baptized and saved by accepting Jesus Christ as your personal Lord and Savior. It wasn't possible to experience the favor of God if you weren't covered by the blood of Jesus for the remission of sins. This would keep you from the temptation and torment of the devil, as well as stay you from the lake of fire forever.

This doctrine was masterful at keeping you from things. And I'd never questioned it until I made the visit to Japan. Before my trip, the heavy clouds of judgment and my own staunch beliefs always won out against any uncertainty or inquiry. Soon things began to swirl out of control in my mind, and finding answers to my questions became more important than ever before. This time, I'd at least sit long enough with myself to allow the feeling inside to speak its truth.

Asking the Hard Questions

I'd been baptized at the age of 13, becoming a full-fledged member of my family's church and verbally committing my life to the service of Jesus Christ. This was the only spiritual truth, the only way of being, I'd ever known.

But after being in Japan for a month and becoming fast friends with those who practiced Buddhism, my religious commitment sat in question at the alter of my mind. I finally had to ask:

If Jesus is the only way to heaven, then what about my Buddhist friends in Japan? Can I have friends of different faiths? What will this say about me and my beliefs as a Christian?

These questions became frightening. My hands would sweat at the thought of having to be honest with myself about the answers that might arise. It was inevitable, though. I had to know what I really believed at my core. It felt as if my very life depended upon it.

But even as I questioned, I had to admit to myself that my spirit already knew the answers to what my mind was agonizing over.

I was lying on my bed in my Harlem apartment talking to my roommate about the upcoming summer when a thought came to my mind.

"If God created us all, then why are some going to heaven and some to hell?" I blurted out.

He stared at me strangely, before asking me to explain. This question had been constantly racing through my mind day and night after my return from Japan. I couldn't understand why, in the middle of whatever I might be doing at a given moment, this thought would break into my mind.

My roommate and I had discussions about God and Jesus often. Both of us were secure in our religious conviction and had claimed to be devout Christians. This had been a tacit prerequisite with regard to my relationships and friendships, dating all the way back to the time of my baptism at 13.

I didn't pursue the conversation with my roommate any further. I let it go and continued on talking about something else. But the uncertainty dogged me, and the anxiety around the questions in my mind continued to mount. I'd often wake up in the morning with my brain cluttered with unspoken questions.

I recall getting so frustrated that I yelled out loud in my apartment, "Why is it so important for me to find an answer to this?"

Then one day, while riding the 'A' train back uptown to my apartment, a word in bold letters printed on an advertisement flashed, like a strobe effect, before my eyes: L-O-V-E. Out of all the books I'd read and scriptures I'd heard quoted about Jesus, the one theme describing who and what Jesus was all about was LOVE.

"What is love?" I asked quietly to myself as I rode further uptown. "What does it really mean?"

I brooded over the question all the way home from the subway station. I'd heard the word used millions of times. I'd used it quite a bit myself. I'd unknowingly chosen the word as a staple of my vocabulary. Growing up it was deemed honorable to tell someone, "I love you." In Sunday school each week, Mrs.

Tennie Mae Redd would stand up and point to the words written on the chalkboard, "God Is Love" as we recited them.

I realized that saying "I love you" had become somewhat of a formality with me. Because I wished favor and friendship from everybody I came into contact with, I'd often finish my final sentence of the conversation with, "I love you." It's not that there wasn't truth to my saying this, but most of the time I had used it to appear a certain way in order to get the approval I so desperately thought I needed. Even people with whom I had vague or short-lived encounters often heard verbal expressions of love from me, though I didn't have an authentic feeling of love for them inside. Instead of being conscious of what I was saying, my gesture became a part of my intellect rather than an intention of my heart.

Now I was finally stopping to ask, "What is love?"

It seemed like an elementary question. However, I intuitively understood that delving into this question would require nothing short of a total transformation of the way I viewed life and its meaning in my day-to day existence. To truly have an understanding of the nature of love, beyond mere emotionality, is to understand that which is at the core of humanity. Love is the source of all creation, the dynamic, eternal force at the center of our Universe.

All creation. Not just some of creation. Not just the parts of creation that attended my church or agreed with the doctrines of my denomination. All creation.

I chose not to think so much about what I'd been told about love. Instead, I decided to reflect on the feeling tone. My mind turned to my childhood, where I'd been more free and open to life. But even while imagining those carefree, happy times, I found myself feeling betrayed. I was starting to question everything about my religious beliefs. At one point, I even felt like I'd almost been tricked into believing religious principles that suddenly felt flawed and somewhat immature.

I contemplated my mother, who was the face of unconditional love for me. She was quick to tell me that she loved me, but I felt her love way before she ever uttered the words. No matter what I did—good or bad—my mother always showered me with something that I could only describe as God. Her expression was never attached to any specific action, and neither did it withhold its beauty based on expectations. I could see this presence in her eyes, her gestures, her posture, and even in her most challenging moments of disappointment. It was strong and active.

From there, my awareness expanded out beyond myself to encompass the hearts of others, both people I knew and people I'd never met before. Love resonated within me deeper than I'd ever experienced it, bringing on tears of gratitude. Rather than relying on an intellectual understanding, I wanted to embody the insight that love dissolved limitations. Nothing—not color, religion, gender, sexual persuasion, or anything else—could stand against the power of love. This presence embraced everyone, no matter what the circumstance or condition.

Love was everywhere. And, for the first time, I could feel that.

These insights encouraged me to take full responsibility for the choices I'd made in my life with regard to my religious beliefs. In hindsight, the notion of separating people because of different religious doctrines and affiliations seemed ridiculous.

Ultimately, this separation has become a platform to keep us from fully loving and embracing one another as human beings. I'm completely convinced that this isn't what Jesus was about at all. It's still my personal belief that Jesus Christ healed the sick, laid hands on those in need, and performed miracles, just as each and every one of us has also been commissioned to do. But Jesus's main mission was to love—to show love, to act love, to be love—no matter what. For me, he remains the greatest exemplar of love that has ever walked the earth, leaving a blueprint on how to treat one another.

It became clear to me that, rather than using Jesus's example as a reason to condemn or exclude others who believed differently than I did, I'd been called to use Jesus's example to perfect the nature of love within my own being. Jesus's name was to be the mantra forever on my lips, exhorting me to give love freely and unconditionally on every step of my journey through this life.

The Depths of Understanding

Armed with this deeper understanding, I expanded the scope of my questions. Again, I asked myself: If Jesus is love, then why are some of us going to heaven, while others go to hell? Is there a heaven and a hell? Do I believe in a heaven and a hell? Where am I going to spend eternity? Can my Buddhist friends come with me? What about Muslims, Hindus, Jews, and all the other people of all the other religions in the world?

I often whispered these questions to myself, because I still wasn't completely comfortable with asking them out loud. Even posing such questions internally was a big step for me. In prior years, I would've immediately aborted any such thoughts for fear of blaspheming against God. But these inquiries couldn't be avoided now. This was a soul mandate. I had to know.

The more questions I asked, the more confused I seemed to become. In my eight years living in New York, I could count on two hands the number of times I attended church. This was abnormal behavior for me. I could count on one hand the number of times I missed going to either Sunday school or Sunday-morning service while growing up.

After many hours spent in silence, I became frustrated again and reverted back to playing the blame game. I concluded that my parents had lied to me and even that Jesus had lied to me. I chose to close all channels to Christianity and any doctrine I'd grown up with until I could sort things out about what, and whom, I really believed in.

At one point, just prior to making this decision, I attended a high-spirited Pentecostal church in Harlem. But after 45 minutes, I walked out and never returned. It was obvious that I was looking for my next spiritual evolution. I just didn't know what it was. Feeling empty, with the voices of confusion and anger running rampant in my mind, I vowed to find an outlet for my spiritual growth.

Most church services lasted past my 12:30 p.m. call time at the theater on Sundays anyway. So I used this as a great excuse as to why I didn't need to attend church. Joining the cast of *The Lion King* became a pleasant replacement for attending Sunday-morning services. The words, the story, and the music provided me with spiritual upliftment. The story is about a father who loved his son so much that even after his untimely and haunting death, he resurfaces to remind the son of who he is in the grand scheme of things. His spirit admonishes the son to fulfill his destiny, giving him the courage to take his rightful place as king of the Pridelands. What I saw throughout this show was the manifestation of the greatest gift one could ever give or embody: Love.

Over time, as I became more and more acquainted with the voice of Spirit operating within me, it became clear that the belief in duality and separation that I'd always held had become a feeding ground for the voices of ego. These chattering voices, full of confusion and judgment, tried to keep a stranglehold on my growth. In my understanding of the teachings of Jesus, this was the exact opposite of what he admonished people to be and do.

The chattering voices of negativity that so often attempt to run our lives cannot continue to hold dominion when faced with the truth of the Universal power of oneness and love. Judgment, ridicule, anger, resentment, unforgiveness, fear, and separation all fade when confronted with the pure light of truth. And the truth is that unconditional love is not just for some of us. It's here to be experienced by all of us—because it's the divine nature of who and what we are. When the voice of intuition speaks through us, it's the voice of unconditional love that we're hearing.

Chapter 14

The Voice Will Always Remind Us of Who and What We Are

The Choice

The voice that matters will always lead you toward your greater good and the unfolding of your life's purpose. But we all have the choice of listening or not listening, heeding or not heeding its wisdom. When we listen, we release the distractions that pull us away from learning about our purpose. Distractions sap our energy and take our mind off the moment. We get caught up in doing things, while forgetting that it's not what we do—it's why we do what we do that defines our purpose.

Whatever you do, when it's done with the intention of inspiring and benefitting others, that generosity becomes a blessing that travels through you and channels life-giving energy to other people. It's freeing to know that you're making a difference and that the difference is changing the world. Conversely, when one hoards one's good from others, it speaks volumes about a consciousness steeped in scarcity and separation. The long-term effects of this selfishness can lead to the type of spiritual stagnation that keeps the individual from experiencing the abundance of life.

When you listen to the chattering, selfish voice of the ego, you'll find that it gets bored very easily and always wants to know what's in it for *it* in any given situation. But the voice of guidance is constantly reminding us to remember our truth: that we are both the divine gift and the giver, here to share with the world from a consciousness of overflowing abundance.

In order to keep this at the forefront of my mind, I say a prayer of gratitude and willingness. I offer this prayer to you now, to use as a guide as you continue forward on the path of remembering who you really are and why you're here in this place, at this moment in time:

"I am here to serve. I am here to be a blessing to everyone that I come into contact with by sharing my gifts. That might happen through music, teaching, art, healing, dancing, writing, speaking, and even a gentle smile. There are as many different ways for this blessing to occur as there are people willing to share their truth. Today, I willingly show up as the face of God. I will, to the best of my ability, create my life with that in the forefront of my intention. I will leave nothing on the stage of life when I am done—not one unfilled note, not one precious moment. I will present and share my work as burning alms before God, consumed by the fire of joy and refinement. To that end, I will be the "everything" that I have come to the planet to be, always aspiring to show the magnificent, unfathomable face of the divine intelligence. This is my face and the face of everyone that

I meet. And together we truly are the world, connected to all that exists within. Amen."

Exercise

Close your eyes and take a deep breath. Think about all that you've been given and tell yourself, "Thank you." Bring to mind a particular occasion that gave you joy. Maybe it was being hired for your first job or being selected to be part of something that you deemed special or important. Now, in your attitude of gratitude, be thankful for everything—that which seems good and that which doesn't seem so good. Continue to breathe it all in as goodness. Now, as you exhale, be conscious of breathing the goodness out to make room for more to come in.

Depression Vs. Refinement

Regardless of the circumstance, the voice of higher intention is always walking us through the tough times so that we can see through the film of separation into the reality of oneness. This guiding hand is necessary, because it's so easy to forget who we really are during the times of hardship that pop up in all of our lives. But the voice that speaks to us and within us never forgets. It constantly beckons us to break out of the confinements of circumstance and look with fresh eyes at the true nature of reality.

It's part of the human experience to go through some dark, uncomfortable moments in life. These dark periods are essential and necessary. Experiences of sadness, loss, or depression don't surface to serve as metaphorical pitchforks meant to torment you, but rather as tuning forks that help refine you. In other words, we don't encounter hardships for the sake of suffering, but for the sake of growth; they're preparation for activation into a higher level of being. When we choose to look at ourselves from this broader perspective, it opens the channel to hear the voice of guidance more clearly. As we mature spiritually and emotionally, the sound of the voice broadcasting its message becomes pleasing to our ears, regardless of the trials that may be accompanying it.

There's a divine connection between depression and inspiration. Most people see depression as an ordeal to be denied, hidden, or endured in some level of shame. But I believe that we must re-term depression. These times of darkness are growing pains. The circumstances that we're living with may be changing. Things that we love and believe that we need may be falling away or disappearing. But our willingness to stand firmly in our place, while remaining in a state of non-resistance, creates an opening for expanded awareness to blossom. Strength, wisdom, compassion, flexibility, courage, determination, and other qualities of that nature show up as bigger and better expressions of our divine humanity.

The new identity being birthed within us during this process is what becomes the spontaneous kinetic energy of inspiration. The seeds that we've planted flower and grow. We have the ability to be inspired at all times, no matter what's happening in the world of circumstance. However, we must honestly decide what we want to experience. We chose our experiences, but we don't control them. Release the need to control, and know that the power of who and what you are makes room for inspired thought to catapult you beyond the experience. Allow the space for grace to take over. Consider adjusting your thought process to, "This is a growth cycle," rather than, "This is a depression cycle." See what gifts stem from the ability to stay open through adversity.

It's never too late to surrender to your next wave of goodness. Even in the midst of the most devastating circumstance, the voice is broadcasting the message that can propel you into your well-being. It's up to the individual to choose whether he or she wants to hang back and get sucked deeper into misery, or jump into the flow of life. You don't have to worry about knowing intellectually what to do. The instructions are contained in the flow. The answers are in the present moment.

Let source energy flow through you like the air you breath through your nostrils. Give until there's nothing left, knowing that as one miracle unfolds another awaits its course through and as you. Be the voice that matters—always creating a world that works for every living thing.

The Task of Validating from Within

Too often, people depend upon something or somebody to validate them. It's out of a belief in separation from the Source that one continues to search for answers in exterior places. Don't get me wrong, we're all inspired by what we see—the vibrant color of a flower, a singer sustaining a "money note" on television, or listening to a philanthropist speak about his or her efforts to help humankind. All of these things can bring about an impulse to be part of this unfolding that's so potent that it causes us to consider new ways to expand our contributions. However, caution should be taken, knowing that these outside sources of information cannot always be relied upon, especially when what's required is the inside job of raising self-awareness.

Most of the time, these outside sources and influences know nothing of the details of your particular path. Far too many times people implement parameters for their lives that have been set with another person's experience in mind. I, too, have fallen victim to the trap of waiting for others to tell me I was okay, that I was brilliant enough to fulfill a task, that I was on the pathway to finding excellence. The insecurity that gripped much of my adolescence spilled over into my early years of adulthood, completely drowning the validating voice of intuition and guidance. Sure, the impulse for us to be encouraged by someone else's achievements and journey is natural and necessary. But the desire to participate in your unfolding good is directly related to your feelings about the vital nature of what you are here to do and the light you have come to shine.

There Are Always Exceptions to the Rule

It's not all the time that you should permit your actions to be dictated by the beat of another's drum. But when you're in the company of sages and those seasoned in life, such individuals can provide healthy and wonderful exceptions. Words of wisdom coming from a saint (as we used to call them) provided the moral foundation for the entire community when I was young. If you were ever in a jam, you could call on something you'd heard from one of these sages to encourage you at that moment and, out of nowhere, it seemed, a pearl of wisdom would come to mind.

My mother often spoke of a woman by the name of Creasy Martin, a beloved woman, born a slave in the mid 1800s, who became known for her far-fetched stories, prophetic words, and mystical readings in the tiny community of Lake Providence. Aunt Creasy, as she was affectionately called, was a fair-skinned woman with a wide, prominent nose and not a tooth to be seen in her mouth. Though not gifted with book smarts, she was well seasoned with wisdom even beyond the 80 years that she lived. Her forte: Storytelling.

Aunt Creasy loved children as much as she loved settling into a rhythm to tell one of her juicy, old-fashioned tales. My mother and the other children of the community often found themselves sitting wherever they could find room to listen as Aunt Creasy showered anecdotes and stories upon their little heads. To them, she was more than just an old, snaggle-toothed griot. Her posture of wisdom and charismatic tone captivated the youngsters' imaginations, and even the interest of the more mature adults in the neighborhood. As Aunt Creasy spoke, she sounded just like a self-possessed Southern Baptist preacher on Sunday morning, hitting every note while mesmerizing the impressionable minds in front of her, including my mother. Aunt Creasy's stories transported my mother to a place of make-believe, far from the feeble-framed, well-kept house that she and her seven brothers and sister called home.

"There's gon' be streetlights here one day," my mother recalled Aunt Creasy telling the children. "And you see these here dirt paths? They gon' all be paved. And through this lil community is gon' run a main artery through the city of Nashville. All around is gon' be buildings and schools and hospitals." How and where she received this information was beyond normal thinking, and according to my mother, every one of Aunt Creasy's predictions came to pass.

My mother distinctly recalled an occasion when she and other children in the community were all sitting, listening to the old woman embellish another one of her tall tales, when Aunt Creasy suddenly stopped her banter in midsentence to make a request of her enchanted audience.

"Look up in the sky, chil'ren. You see that der star? I want you to reach up there and grab it and put it in your mouth."

Aunt Creasy pretended to snatch a star from the sky and gobble it up. My mother, who was a feisty child, refused.

"I'm not pickin' no star out of the sky and eatin' it!" my mother insisted.

"Grab that star, I say!" Aunt Creasy exclaimed.

"No!" my mother stubbornly insisted.

After a few rounds, Aunt Creasy's persistence would finally convince my mother to play along.

"Now you done ate the star, how do you feel, chil'ren?" she asked.

Not waiting for a response, Aunt Creasy tilted her head back, clasped her wrinkled hands together, and then threw her arms open wide.

"Good," she crowed, "because you all gon' be stars one day."

Aunt Creasy laughed and walked away, her face full of joy. The children watched as she gingerly made her way through the brush and fields on her journey back home.

Aunt Creasy's ability to tap into the mystical vastness, something far greater than the religious doctrine she'd known all her life, was more than evident. The old woman was, undeniably, tuned in to a higher frequency. She communed with a divine source that not only gave her insight to the future of her small, beloved community, but sparked a mystic relationship with the celestial nature of her own being. She understood herself to be a luminous star, and because she saw that light in herself, she was also able to recognize it in the eyes of even the smallest child. Her words to children like my mother were so magical and important because they corresponded with divine truth inherent within each of them.

My mother admitted to me that as she grew to understand what Aunt Creasy's admonishment meant, her life was profoundly altered. And, just like Aunt Creasy, my mother shared stories with my siblings and me that caused us to stop and reflect and search for that intuitive grandeur within. It's that place that knows only love, creativity, peace, and wholeness in its purest form. It is always prepared to shine and reflect its genius.

While she was cleaning around the house, I could hear my mother mumble to herself, "I'm gonna step out on faith," and "I'm believing solely in God!" She never knew that I could hear her, but her words not only echoed in my internal ear, they seemed to become ingrained in my DNA. And as I grew older, whenever I felt like I needed an emotional boost, these words would rush to the forefront of my mind, acting as an access door to the power of guidance that is always calling us to be more than who and what we think we are.

Aunt Creasy changed the lives of those she came into contact with because she was open and willing enough to engage the spontaneous voice that told her to jump up and catch a star. She, without question, played out her part and insisted that the group join her. In that present moment was a gift; the present was the gift. In a moment of impulsive brilliance when an old woman surrendered to the childlike laughter of the divine, she gave a few little hearts a taste of a world of possibility. She challenged them to self-identify with something brilliant and eternal. Because Aunt Creasy heard the call of the voice within, my mother heard it as well. And because my mother heard, I heard it, too.

When we allow it, the voice moves us into action and finally into embodying that which we have been called to manifest and demonstrate. Like Aunt Creasy said, "We're here to be like those stars in the sky. We're here to shine!"

In This Moment

I'm sure that most of you have heard the phrase, "The moment is all we have." This is one of the simplest and greatest truths that I've heard. The only moment that will ever be available to us is the moment we're experiencing right now. Within this moment lives the possibility of having a life-altering experience. Instead of looking for miracles out there somewhere or hoping for things to get better sometime "in the future," accept the truth that miracles are constantly showing up in our lives and that the future can never be more than what we're creating it to be today. All throughout my life, I've heard great spiritual teachers echo Aunt Creasy, saying, "Shine chil'ren, shine. Shine the light of heaven, chil'ren. You are the light of the world!"

The shining star in the sky is always reflecting back the same magnificence and pure beauty described by the eyes of its beholder—you! There's a voice reminding you that there are occasions you may have overlooked or forgotten that have the ability to serve as a platform in your next encounter with greatness.

The End of the Road

We're going to stop and imagine living our lives backward. Pretend that you're at the end of your journey in this particular human manifestation. As you survey your life, what are you finding? How do you feel about the life you lived? Did you achieve your heart's desires? If so, how did you get there? (If not, why not? What paths can you reimagine taking that would allow you to fulfill your purpose?) Would you have made other choices in getting from point A to point B? What will you want people to say with regard to the life you lived here on planet Earth? What were the themes of your life? How did they affect human kind? Did you exude excellence in your endeavors and realize your vast potential? What platforms did you use to demonstrate you talents and share your gifts? Was it all worth the hard work? What mattered most to you at the end of the day?

The purpose of this exercise is to have an opportunity to understand that you have the creative power to craft your life in any way you'd like it to be. The way to know the outcome is by putting things into place now that will yield the type of life and outcome you wish to experience. It's my experience that the Universe will handle all the details, and that they should be the least of your concerns. Remaining awake and aware in each moment so that your attention remains focused on your intention is what gets you to the desired end place.

No matter how life looks to you at this point, there's a great opportunity to call forth, acknowledge, and embrace the unfolding that's prepared to catapult you into a world of infinite possibility. Your life can begin anew right now. You don't have to wait until times get better or when you have enough money or when you have finally finished your dissertation and get your Ph.D. The good life is ready right now.

I find this exercise very interesting. As soon as I begin to write down or even think about my life from this point of reference, my entire perspective adjusts to what I say. My body begins to take on a different posture when I say, "Philanthropy took me to parts of the world I never knew existed" and "When the headlines read that the water supply flowing into that African village and that Indian city was no longer filled with toxic, bacteria-laden waste, but with clean water, I knew my part in the 'clean water' initiative had made a difference."

I even see myself describing it with a certain tone of voice and twinkle in my eye. The list can be endless, but you'll know what really resonates with you, so there won't be a need to jot down every aimless aspiration. In your heart of hearts, you already know what you want to do and become to make the world a place that works for everyone.

Once you've played your life backward, take a list of your accomplishments, and see how many of those items had the intention of being a benefit to the local and extended community, the nation, and the world.

Chapter 15

And the Two Shall Become One

Embracing the Holy Song: Some Final Thoughts...

I don't care what people have said about you or how many times you've been told that you can't do something or that your life will never amount to anything. It doesn't matter if you grew up in a dysfunctional family or your parents never told you that they loved you. It doesn't even matter if you don't have a clue who your parents were. Conversely, it also doesn't matter how many people have told you how special you are and that they're counting on you or how many outside expectations you've been buried under.

I'm not interested in how much money you may have or how many cars you own—if your financial portfolio calculates somewhere between zero or a billions dollars. You may think the weight of the world is on your shoulders and that everybody is out to get you or do harm to you. Many people in your life may have disappointed you by saying they would help and support you, but didn't. None of that is important. It's all part of your story, the chatter that seeks to make you believe that the future is destined to be based on the mishaps of the past. But, once again, none of that is true.

As you awaken and tune in to the voice of truth within, you'll come to understand that your contribution to the unfolding good taking place in this Universe is far greater than any trial or tribulation you'll ever face. I am persuaded that if you haven't already become well acquainted with your gift to humanity, now is the perfect time that you do.

Remember, our charge is to become the spiritual qualities that we want to see taking place on our planet right now. Peace. Love. Joy. Courage. Inspiration. This means stepping into your truth with such conviction that nothing can stand in the way of you fulfilling your highest purpose. The voice that matters—the voice of guidance and highest intention—is the medium by which we can access any virtue we wish to experience and demonstrate. The only way to access this voice is through an exploration of the soul, an inspection of the heart, and a few courses in truth and honesty.

Someone may have forgotten that there's an inner voice desiring to get his or her attention. Someone else may not have known that it ever existed—this thing I call the intuitive prophet. This voice gently taps on our heads and hearts to remind us of our initial plan, our primary intention. Sure, circumstances may seem a bit harsh at times. You may experience some awful situations. But even then the voice of compassion and grace is there to support your recovery back to peace and love.

Once you say yes to the call and begin to actively participate in its unfolding, you'll begin to realize that what you've come to embody, share, and impart on the planet is much more than your state of affairs will ever be. Fear and doubt can never measure up to the words that the deep inner self is speaking. Money and all material possessions in the world couldn't begin to scratch the surface of our divine mandate. Heeding this mandate will no doubt lead you on a journey to reveal the secrets of your soul's desires.

The fear and discontent of the egoic voice isn't nearly powerful enough to stop you from succeeding on this path, though believe me, it will continue to try. "You're not smart enough." "They don't like you." "That's a stupid way of thinking." "You're funny looking." "Don't act like that." "Don't talk like that." "That's a crazy idea." "That's too hard for you." "You can't learn that." "You weren't meant to be in that profession." "Time isn't on your side."

The laundry list of limiting words and phrases can seem endless, sometimes becoming the definitive standards within our thought process. But you no longer have to listen to these meddling voices. You can choose higher. The creative genius inside of you is at your beck and call every waking moment that you are breathing. It lets you know that it's ready to create something in your life beyond your wildest dreams.

All of the help that you need to achieve your greatest dreams is all around you. All you have to do is ask, and it is given. If you look for it, you'll find it. Of course, it's going to take work, but that part of the process is mandatory. Living from the inside out is the only way of fulfilling the mandate. By becoming one with self, you enhance the possibility of attracting all of the good that you've been looking for.

Every single thing you need to fulfill your purpose is all inside of you. You already have it. As a matter of fact, you came here with it. Remember, we're here to facilitate one another's journey in finding these inner treasures.

I champion Aunt Creasy's words: "Shine chil'ren, shine!"

It's time to reveal the luster. That is what I am choosing to do. I came to shine the light, the light that lights the world … and so did you.

I still have some layers to go. I suspect that I'll always be in the mode of peeling back and letting go. It's part of an unending process, because the uncovering forever calls us into action. The voice is always transmitting messages. It never fades. It continuously seeks to transmit its message in order that we awaken to our highest good. The voice of spirit has neither a beginning nor an end. As we have seen, we all have the ability to hear it, feel it, see it, and experience its power and instruction in a way that we understand. The question is whether we're willing to listen. Listening and hearing are two distinctly different things. We can hear and not heed the message. When we're willing to listen and adhere to the instructions that we receive, life is forever changed. My prayer is that we continue to awaken to the call and divine purpose.

The process of waking up to the vastness inside of us is, in itself, a beginning point from which we can truly live this thing called life. As we become steadfast, the voice of guidance kicks into high gear, becoming stronger and clearer. We hear through the fog of our mental chatter, the voice's signal to continue to remember the truth of who we are.

As we soar on this magnificent journey, we'll fly into turbulent winds and even drastic weather and storms at times. But there are great blessings within the storms. When we get a really good rain here in Los Angeles, it cleanses the air of smog and debris. After the storm passes, we can see things that at once appeared to be far away as if they are within an arm's reach. It's funny what a little cleansing rain can do. The trees and flowers seem more vibrant and lush. The air quality becomes more conducive to the health and wholeness of our bodies as it rushes through the lungs. Even the energy of the city heightens, inducing us to become more playful and less stressful.

Our storms are like healing showers that can eventually wash away old habits and ways of being if we let them. Doing so inevitably makes room for new growth.

The voice also lets us know that attitude is a key to our experience. When we choose the more affirmative and constructive course, we invite our experiences, whether favorable or not, to reveal the lessons. For example, I chose not to get upset and call it quits when my car was stolen. Instead, I affirmed that I was supposed to be in Los Angeles and that the timing for my arrival could not have been more perfect. What seemed to be a setback actually turned out to be a setup by the Universe. In choosing to encourage myself, I subsequently gave myself the opportunity to experience life in a whole new and wonderful way.

As we continue to listen to the voice, the principles that we've explored become more than just ideas or things. They take on a dynamic manifestation as the life of every person that actively participates in his or her spiritual, mental, and emotional unfolding. The embodiment of these themes becomes the lifeline through which we all can experience the joy and beauty of transcendent living.

As you wake up to the gifts that you're on the planet to give, you'll begin to realize that what you previously believed was "your thing" is really a gift to the world. At that point, you may find your intention shifting. Whereas before, you may only have thought about yourself and your family, you find that you can't help but keep your brothers and sisters all over the world in mind. The fire burns brighter than it ever has The possibilities for your life continue to propel you into your greater good and buoy your intent to make an indelible imprint on the world.

Don't flinch if you feel the fire becoming hotter. Notice the brightness of the flame. You have stepped into another ring of divine power. Stand in your authority. There's power in your knowing that where you are is exactly where you're meant to be—on time and perfect. The voice of the higher self is always inviting you to step into its center and become one with its blazing light. This circle of consuming fire is like no other entity; although it takes you over, it never distorts the essence of its gift, a burning away of that which know longer serves you. The old falls away and disintegrates, as a new glow radiates from within.

The new glow, a flame ready to serve the present unfolding, is so bright that it becomes contagious, a new standard of excellence. This vibrant blaze is you. It becomes you, and you become one with it. The voice will guide you through all of this, if you will listen. Are you ready?

As soon as you heed the voice of intuition and guidance, whether you're conscious of your actions or not, you give universal intelligence permission to do what it does best: Create a platform for you to awaken to your greatest potential. Each step out into your path's unchartered territory is a declaration of trust that continues to strengthen the marriage between your soul's destiny and the divine creative force.

I knew when I chose to heed the voice I heard in my dressing room in Atlanta, which instructed me to leave the comforts of all that I'd known and move to New York, that this was not a passing fancy. I had no idea what I had stepped into, nor did I have a clue as to how things would unfold. But the part of my being that had always longed to trust itself, the part that only knows how to trust, leapt out like a star in the night. It knew. It knew that something greater than I'd ever experienced awaited me—something that logic and intellect had no words for.

Of course, a large part of my psyche remained arrested and grounded by the pain of past experiences and discouraging words. There were voices all around offering nothing but ridicule and discouragement. Even those closest to me, who wanted only the best for me, at times fell into this trap.

"Before you go to New York, I want you to do me a favor," my mother had said. "I would like for you to go see a psychiatrist and let him examine your head. I believe you're going crazy!"

My mother was serious. She insisted that I see a shrink. But what my mother (and everyone else, for that matter) could not have known was that the mere thought of leaving for the bright lights of Broadway had elicited emotions from me that could only be rivaled by the feeling I felt as I danced when I was a five-year-old child. I kept quiet about my intentions, but never allowed anyone else to change them. In silence, I was able to give full attention to what I was hearing.

As I stepped into what I visualized in my mind, I began to actively participate in its unfolding. In that same way, may you be ignited to be fully present to what the voice is instructing you to do in your own life.

I want you to try another exercise with me.

Get in a comfortable position. Sitting with your back straight, close your eyes and take a deep breath. Set the intention that the old, surface way of thinking is being burned away from your conscious and subconscious mind. Visualize this happening with each breath and, as it does, usher in a new level of awareness. See yourself walking in your power and in the fullness of your heart's desire.

Memories of the past may come to the surface. Some of these images recall experiences and people that you would have rather forgotten. Remember that these visual markers never come to torment or persecute us. Rather, they come to point the way as we continue to stay in the flow of life's awakening. As we recondition our minds to embrace (rather than run from) any discomfort or regret that may arise, we set the stage for true healing and understanding. The seeds of wholeness that were always present, even during our most painful encounters, transform the ache of past wounds into a sage's lesson—flourishing words of wisdom that lift and expand everything and everyone.

Be prepared to continue to revisit themes such as forgiveness and surrender at every turn. These glorious pruning shears can appear at a moment's notice to cut away the deadweight that would otherwise hinder us from moving through life with ease and grace at our side to guide us.

The qualities of ease and grace became stalwarts in my vocabulary during the preparation of this book. As these words continued to penetrate my own soul, they brought me to new edges of awareness and growth. This tremendous surge of conscious energy stood in stark contrast to all the times when I'd tried to do things my way and make it happen.

I remember working on a very important CD project a long time ago. Instead of relaxing, letting go, and allowing myself to be guided toward the graceful completion of the work, I became extremely overprotective of what had been created. I retreated in fear and doubt, which in effect blocked the creative energy from moving through the process. Instead of releasing what I'd already created, I began adhering to old patterns that centered on control and self-sabotage. The constriction was manifest in every area of my life. I stopped tithing. I began cutting short conversations with friends. My eating habits became erratic (those pieces of pumpkin pie at my favorite restaurant, Urth Café, became meals instead of rationed dessert). I became reclusive, not wanting to listen to anybody or anything, including the inner voice.

I recall screaming out in disgust one afternoon, "What do you want? What do you want from me?"

I don't remember the details of the situation that caused the outburst, but the collision of these two opposite ways of moving through life (listening to the voice as opposed to doing it all myself, my way) had left me at a very painful crossroads. I remember trying to calmly breathe through a piercing stream of chatter before finally surrendering. Standing on the solid ground of surrender and silence, I asked questions about my next steps. And I got answers. They weren't the answers I thought I was going to hear, but they were exactly what I needed to hear.

At many points in this ongoing process, you may feel like you're losing you mind. It may seem as if you're alone. Times may appear so dire that it seems like all of your thoughts are desperate or full of fear. These thoughts, just like a summer storm, are only passing through. It's during these times that you can remember the victories and triumphant strides you've made in arriving to your present state and know confidently that this too shall pass.

Again, learning to consciously breathe through any situation that arises will give you access to the peace only found in the inner dialogue with the soul. Like the furious northeasterly storm that hit New York City on the night I lost my wallet, things can seemingly pile on and freeze, leaving you to believe that the problem you may be facing is forever without resolution. But the act of conscious breathing frees you up to listen to the voice of intention, while simultaneously casting your vibration to higher ground. Through these situations, you realize that when you think you've lost something, you haven't lost anything. You've actually gained an opportunity to become more in tune with your authentic nature—rediscovering and communing with the power that lies within.

Make no mistake about it; there's always a party going on. You can choose to participate or not. If you show up at the party, will you be brave enough to get out onto the middle of the floor and dance? Can you decide not to timidly stand on the wall, feeling the intoxicating pulse, while watching everybody else having the time of their lives? Will you put your drink down long enough to set your body in motion?

I realize that some people haven't awakened to the fact that this heavy, burdensome thing called life is actually a beautiful party—and it's calling you to dance! Life is calling you to be free enough to hear the music in your heart that's playing your favorite tune. If you show up to the party, I'm sure that you'll hear the beat calling to you. For everyone, the beat is different. Sure, the beat may take on another rhythm while you're in mid-stride, but just like any beautiful piece of music, the tune sound is never expected to stay the same. Life is about change.

There's always a new song of discovery and possibility ringing in the air. Once you lift your head and hear the music playing, you become able to bypass the intellect and delve into the magic and synchronicities that occur when one slips into the flow of life. This process will never end. It takes a continuous commitment to surrendering, in rapt attention, to the song that's moving through you.

Just the other day I was noticing how things are rapidly changing in my life. Things that for years I was passionately interested in seemed to be fading, making room for new possibilities. I took particular notice when I woke up one morning and, after meditation, decided that I didn't have to be on Broadway again. Since leaving New York and *The Lion King,* I'd always had in my mind that I'd one day return to do another show. When this thought came to me, I didn't even cringe. I thought it about it for a moment to see how it resonated, and afterward said, "Wherever I'm supposed to be is where I'll be in love with life. If I never grace another Broadway stage, I'll forever be grateful and complete for the time I had the honor of being there."

The shift didn't stop there—my relationships, friendships, career choices, and spiritual practices seem to be changing over night. As I closed these chapters, the losses felt emotionally draining. However, unlike other moments when I'd experienced dark nights of the soul, this time I quickly recognized what was happening. I remembered that just a few months prior to these radical changes, I began spiritually releasing people, things, and conditions from my life, and surrendering to what was emerging. Those pruning shears were sharp; however, they knew how to cut in a way that fostered new growth and didn't impair it.

When you go through a deep cleansing and there's a great falling away, circumstances can feel like they're coming at you fast and furious. You may think you don't have the proper facility to move with the new sound, which may feel cacophonic and disturbing at times. But have no fear. Never doubt that there's a melody inside of you that instinctively and intuitively hears the subtle beat of your heart. It hears the masterpiece being played by the voice of spirit, the voice of guidance and intuition, which is truly the voice that matters in the evolution of our souls' journey.

As you earnestly seek to know this deep indwelling presence, you'll begin to realize that it, too, is yearning for you. When you meet, like a dazzling couple whose hearts have become one, you and the inner voice shall come to your own sacred agreement by saying yes. For in that moment of soul remembering, you'll understand that you've reconnected with the initial intent of your very existence here on the planet at this most beautiful time. It becomes evident that nothing can ever separate you from your highest potential. The communion with this most inspiring, loving, transforming manifestation of Spirit called the voice that matters is a holy agreement.

It has charmed my path and enlightened my journey, and it is a very present help each and every waking moment.

For you, I pray that it is the same.

"I Am" Produced by Ben Dowling

1. America the Beautiful
2. Tapping
3. I Am
4. Love's In Need
5. Summertime
6. Jesus Loves Me
7. A Place at the Table
8. Seasons of Love
9. In Your Eyes
10. Come Sunday

"Rushing Over Me" Produced by Karlton Taylor & Ben Dowling

1. Rolling River God
2. Narrative
3. Great Is Thy Faithfulness
4. Home
5. My Father's World
6. Narrative
7. God Bless The Child
8. I Forgive Me
9. Give Us This Day
10. My Funny Valentine
11. Use Me

Extraordinary Soul by Charles Holt on AMI

Agape Media International

www.AgapeMe.com

Other Agape Media Artists you may enjoy!

Other Offerings from Agape Media Artists & Authors

Agape Media International (AMI) is dedicated to promoting artists and art forms that uplift the human spirit and inspiring individuals to contribute their own talents to the creation of a world that works for everyone.

Books
Michael Bernard Beckwith | The Answer Is You
Michael Bernard Beckwith | 40-Day Mind Fast Soul Feast
Michael Bernard Beckwith | Life Visioning
Michael Bernard Beckwith | Spiritual Liberation
Cynthia Occelli | Resurrecting Venus
Dianne Burnett | The Road To Reality

Audio Programs by Michael Bernard Beckwith
The Life Visioning Process
The Life Visioning Life Visioning Kit
The Rhythm Of A Descended Master
Your Soul's Evolution
Living From The Overflow

DVDs
The Answer Is You
Spiritual Liberation, the Movie
Superwise Me!
Living In The Revelation

Music CDs
Various Artists | Music From The PBS Special - The Answer Is You
   feat. Siedah Garrett, Will.I.Am, Niki Haris, Rickie Byars Beckwith,
   Agape International Choir
Jami Lula & Spirit In The House / There's A Healin' Goin' On
Charles Holt | I Am
Charles Holt | Rushing Over Me
Rickie Byars Beckwith | Supreme Inspiration
Ester Nicholson | Child Above The Sun
Ben Dowling | The Path Of Peace
Michael Bernard Beckwith / TranscenDance

Inspirational Cards
Life Lift-Off Cards

www.AgapeMe.com

Agape Media YouTube Channel
See videos by Charles Holt, Michael Bernard Beckwith
& other inspirational AMI artists on YouTube:
www.youtube.com/agapemedia